Summing Up

Summing Up

Selected Poems 1962-2022

Dave Oliphant

Copyright © 2024 Dave Oliphant

All Rights Reserved

Lead Editor: Reilly Smith

ISBN: 978-1-962148-05-4
Library of Congress Control Number:2024935321

Manufactured in the United States

Lamar University Literary Press Beaumont, Tx

Dedication

in memory of
my English professors
at then Lamar Tech
1957-1959:
Francis Abernethy
Winfred Emmons
Robert Nossen
Alexander Viner
William Whipple

Recent Poetry from Lamar University Literary Press

Lisa Adams, *Xuai*
Walter Bargen, *My Other Mother's Red Mercedes*
Christine Boldt, *In Every Tatter*
Devan Burton, *A Room for Us*
Jerry Bradley, *Collapsing into Possibility*
Mark Busby, *Through Our Times*
Julie Chappell, *Mad Habits of a Life*
Stan Crawford, *Resisting Gravity*
Glover Davis, *Academy of Dreams*
William Virgil Davis, *The Bones Poems*
Chris Ellery, *Elder Tree*
Dede Fox, *On Wings of Silence*
Alan Gann, *That's Entertainment*
Larry Griffin, *Cedar Plums*
Michelle Hartman, *Irony and Irrelevance*
Lynn Hoggard, *First Light*
Michael Jennings, *Crossings: A Record of Travel*
Gretchen Johnson, *A Trip Through Downer, Minnesota*
Markham Johnson, *Dear Dreamland*
Betsy Joseph & Chip Dameron, *Relatively Speaking*
Ulf Kirchdorfer, *Chewing Green Leaves*
Jim McGarrah, *A Balancing Act*
J. Pittman McGehee, *Nod of Knowing*
Laurence Musgrove, *Bluebonnet Sutras*
Benjamin Myers, *The Family Book of Martyrs*
Janice Northerns, *Some Electric Hum*
Godspower Oboido, *Wandering Feet on Pebbled Shores*
Carol Coffee Reposa, *Sailing West*
Jan Seale, *Particulars*
Steven Schroeder, *the moon, not the finger, pointing*
Glen Sorestad, *Hazards of Eden*
Vincent Spina, *The Sumptuous Hills of Gulfport*
W.K. Stratton, *Betrayal Creek*
Wally Swist, *Invocation*
Ken Waldman, *Sports Page*
Loretta Diane Walker, *Ode to My Mother's Voice*
Dan Williams, *At the Gates, a Refuge of Milkweed and Sunflowers*
Jonas Zdanys, *The Angled Road*

For information on these and other Lamar University Literary Press books go to www.Lamar.edu/literarypress

Acknowledgments

The following poems originally appeared in the respective publications:

"A Texas Version of Crèvecoeur" in *Concho River Review* (Fall 2003)

"Amaya's 'Dixie'" in *The Southern Poetry Anthology*, volume VIII: Texas (Texas Review Press, 2008)

"An Afternoon of Debussy" in *Pulse*, vol. 3, no. 1 (1962)

"Another Hill Country Sunset" in *Between Heaven and Texas*, Poems selected by Naomi Shihab Nye (University of Texas Press, 2006)

"Cedar vs. Live Oak" in *Lightning Key Review*, issue 1.1 (Spring 2014)

"Crawfishing" in *Riata* (Spring 1965)

"Driving Across the Llano Estacado" in *The Dirty Goat*, vol. 20 (2009)

"Ironing at the Colegio Mayor 'Mara'" in *RiverSedge* (Spring 1995)

"Jazz by the Boulevard" in *Red River Review*, no. 49 (November 2013)

"March of the Penguins," "María's Heart," and "Of Burgers & Serpents" in *Sandhill Review* 11 (2010)

"María in Memoriam" in *Travels of a Texas Poet*, vol. 2 (Austin, TX: Alamo Bay Press, 2021)

"María's Hem" in *Langdon Review of the Arts in Texas* (2007-2008)

"María's Smile" in *Ilya's Honey* (Fall 2013)

"María's Voices" in *Latitude 30°18´*, no. 4 (Winter 1985)

"Ode to a '68 VW Bus" in *Red River Review*, no. 50 (Winter 2014)

"Rondo for Mahler" in *The Dirty Goat*, vol. 22 (2010)

"Salado" in *Pax: A Journal for Peace Through Culture* 3, nos. 1 & 2 (1985-1986)

"San Antonio" in *Dactylus*, no. 7 (primavera de 1987)

Some of the poems here are excerpted from multi-section works, like "Teachers at South Park High" and *KD: a Jazz Biography*, but none is included in Dave Oliphant's *The Pilgrimage: Selected Poems, 1962-2012* (Lamar University Literary Press, 2013). All of the poems in the present selection, with the exception of "An Afternoon of Debussy" (winner of the Eleanor Weinbaum Poetry Award), have appeared in one or more of the following books: *Austin* (Austin, TX: Prickly Pear Press, 1985; revised, Alamo Bay Press, 2018, with title changed to *Austin: a Poem*)

Backtracking (Austin, TX: Host Publications, 2004)

The Cowtown Circle (Austin, TX: Alamo Bay Press, 2016)

Footprints, 1961-1978 (Austin, TX: Thorp Springs Press, 1978)

KD: a Jazz Biography (San Antonio, TX: Wings Press, 2012; revised, Alamo Bay Press, 2022)

María's Book (Austin, TX: Alamo Bay Press, 2016)

María's Poems (Austin, TX: Prickly Pear Press, 1987)

Memories of Texas Towns & Cities (Austin, TX.: Host Publications, 2000; revised and expanded, Alamo Bay Press, 2022)

Contents

Backtracking & Other Poems 11
    An Afternoon of Debussy 13
    Crawfishing 16
    Living Room 17
    Backtracking 23
    Ironing at the Colegio Mayor "Mara" 35
    Another Hill Country Sunset 37
    Bert's Barbecue 39
    Vincent at the Wal-Mart Supercenter 43
    A Funeral in Brock Texas 44
    In Upstate New York a Texas Composer Has Lost His Home 46
    A Texas Version of Crèvecoeur 48
    from Teachers at South Park High 50
    Cedar vs. Live Oak 55
    At the Farmers' Market 56
    March of the Penguins 59
    Of Burgers & Serpents 61
    Ode to a '68 VW Bus 62
    DeKalb: 14 February 2008 64
    Bad Day at Black Rock 66
    Driving Across the Llano Estacado 68
    Lone Star Stalag 69
    Elisa's Gift 73
    Donasio Checks the Mail 74
    Amaya's "Dixie" 76
    Girl Gymnasts 77
    Boat House Grill 78
    Jazz by the Boulevard 81
    Rondo for Mahler 83

from *Memories of Texas Towns & Cities* 93
    Woodville 95
    San Antonio 98
    Salado 103
    Paris 108
    Johnson City 109
    from Fort Worth: The Bathroom 111
    The Cowtown Circle 114
    Dallas 127
    Castroville 129
    Burnet 134
    Baird 139

Contents

from *Austin: a Poem*	163
Sabine	165
Red River	182
San Jacinto	193
Nueces	202
from *KD: a Jazz Biography*	215
Prophesying	216
Arriving	225
Zodiacing	238
Expiring	245
from *María's Book*	249
María's Albums	251
María's Dresses	253
María's Genealogy	254
María's Heart	258
María's Hem	260
María's Ideas	261
María's Larkspur	263
María's Maine Coon Cat	266
María's Movies	268
María's New Mexico	272
María's Paint	275
María's Redecoration	276
María's Smile	278
María's Voices	280
María's Yards	287
María in Memoriam (1944-2020)	292

Backtracking & Other Poems

An Afternoon of Debussy

In sleep
he faces
feeling
not seeing
the cracked ceiling
his head
lying at rest
on the soiled pink
pillowcase
her arm extended
beneath the curve of his neck
the baby of five days
reaching its happy hand
toward his rising
sinking
chest

Dressed merely by their child
and a pink sheet
crumpled
from waist to knees
her slender feet
cross in anxiety
ankle on ankle
pale
at the foot of the bed

Half-naked
he daydreams
of two young sparrows:
mates in the
breast-high grass
bowing their heads
this way and that
keeping feathered ears
in touch
with signals of the palsied
wind
in warning
shaking limbs
of a red-&-yellow
Chinese tallow

Sea horses swim
where waves of leaves
mesh
with a soft blue sky
the view inviting
silent eyes
to enter
the tint of the deep
for there pervades
a flaming mouth:
round
a cymbal rolled
through a music
pure
filled with the breath of
life
floating like bubbles
blown from soap
tilting and
by the
    golden tongue
of the sounding sun
glistened
        pink & blue

  breathe
  sonorous strings
   sweep horses
  out to sea

  disarm
  French horns
   the hidden fear
  spread in wings

  readied for flight
  should gleaming notes
   burst
  on the wind in the tree

The child
upon their double base
now plays
the feeding tune

elbowing
vibrating
his manly wire-like hair
waking him at last
his bright blue eyes
on fire

Crawfishing

surrounded now by the shopping center
Black Bridge is where would always go
when just the name was mystery enough
& with its fields of stunted post oaks
the eeriest atmosphere in all Fort Worth
crossing then three sets of railroad tracks
the first saw the trains in the Second War
park awhile as troops threw their candy rations
to all the neighborhood's barefoot kids
who well-supplied with white string & bacon strips
would green-stain their soles on summer's grass
drop lines down their holes to tease them out
& though war is now no longer sweet
& feet are grown sore from awaiting a sale
still nothing is acquired without a catch
the old trestle replaced by this brand-new mall
with its parking-lot moons the pale-blue bait

Living Room

a suite for Louis Zukofsky

1

a fall spree of cuttings

no one around these parts
can stand the way "them
elms sap the soil
from 'lovelier' things"

where they've set them out
is a mystery
to me

one old tree

framed by our picture window
misshapen against
the getting dark

is ugly as a weathered granny
whose beauty lies only
in her hanging on

2

put off for weeks fixing it
the front doorknob
kept ending up
in the hand of
every guest who
"had" to go
an uninvented conversation piece
that gave us all the feeling
of getting caught

3

wondering where they are
not the snows of yesteryears

but all those boys
the loud ones
who kicked their football here
day after day
none around
moved on   must have
like all the others
oil worker families
transferred out
these companies playing

at a game of
God

4

cars carry them by
to cares yes
why
not caresses

5

each evening with this yellow sun
before María
has drawn to
the heavier drapes
I stare
at the near-white
almost gauze-thin curtains
with their two
triangular weaves
divide each square
its woven design
of darker lighter
a yin yang
a warp & woof
roofs
across the street
their colors now
deepened by dusk
I her

6

leaning back in the purplish armchair
big shot like
my gaze going left to right & back
my eyes an adding machine for shadings
of books pamphlets vinyl records
red white & black: races
shapes bindings sizes: nations
spines straight bent: ages
arranged in Uncle Alvin's handmade
handtiqued cases
ways of facing up
including those
have as yet
to get   need   come to
or having
have still
to take in hand
handle
manage
or better yet
to land &
unswayed   unruled
totally to be
inhabited by

7

a little music
a recording then
one chosen from among
composers of
a minor sort
"peripheral" as
one friend aptly
put it
those who
sang it
over again
as the song was all
they
had to sing

8

on one wall a
Picasso print
period: Roman-cubist
titled: 3 musicians

2—Harlequin &
his pal Pierrot—
tricked a Capuchin into
making like

a music stand
a poochy's on the floor
& facing this
María's own open-

mouthed
newsboy
collage
clipped

from print of
a now-yellowed *Harper's Bazaar*
& a cutting from her country's
El Mercurio

held
in the vendor's hand
reading
"till later" in

the language
ever to her green
tongue
native

& at its side
her sister's gift
come by air
sea shells pasted on a board

from the shore they shared
at a silly age

like the one
at 80-odd

holding on
it's said
Picasso still
goes wading

9

:a treatise of

a chewed shoe
a yellow
       measled
               giraffe
     on wheels
angel blue:

toys of a
           boy
           his pet
I would I could

     play upon
           digest in
     an adult
     kind of

          tract:

10

but come back now
to the coffee table

low enough a
support to where
he can walk around the
pot plant (pulling leaves) from
the funeral of his unknown Uncle Tommy

the lamp we've never liked
but bought
& live with
turned on

the map of Chile
land of half our hearts
hanging there on the facing wall
all by night reflected on
gathered upon
the window pane

a life
thinly veiled
framed
until we choose

the moving out
or drawing to of drapes
for the dreaming a space
on into dawn

Backtracking

1

not out of fear that a fork in the road
some turn not taken ended wrongly here
but rather to follow the twists of fate

to see if they are or if it's a matter of choice
to reckon the cost they thought it worth
when it didn't pan out the way they hoped

for it still seems right to remember those
who held to what their minds' eyes saw
though now it's not the same nor even close

far in fact from the dreams bequeathed
regretted half the time as misconceived
the other for having failed to measure up

in spite of all to trace back state by state
harder perhaps on a Texan with little use
for anything arriving from north or east

till swallowing pride head out for lands
some settled before they could later receive
a welcome from these Texas hills & plains

wonder why in Arkansas others failed to stay
where harvested fields of wheat & hay
wear a country boy's home-cut hair

forsaking the miracle of terraced rice
greened by irrigation though only after
had cleared the brush & uprooted trunks

once their plows had broken through
where the John Deeres now stir up the dust
the drivers safe in air-conditioned glassed-in cabs

yoked teams stumbled then on shining clods
now car tires thump on hunks of littered tread
black as the backs of alligators in Cajun swamps

waded through to reach some higher ground
free of crowds at drive-ins another Day's Inn
their search rarely found nor thought to seek

a viola's phrase a verse's measured line
looking more for an unstagnated stream
an uneroded unexhausted terrain

virgin soil for slaves to hoe
for picking cotton until they dropped
then lifted by beer & Memphis blues

but not there yet not even near
when a convoy of trucks in camouflage
khakied troops miles from Joplin's Texarkana

halt at a rest stop erected by public funds
a muscular corporal peeling a pungent orange
while his fellow blacks line up to take their turns

not the relief seasick immigrants were searching for
after perilous passage through sacred burial grounds
down treacherous cliffs into raging creeks

breaking backs over planting plagued by drought
now arrive at the familiar billboards still proclaim
a self-same tasteless fast-food chain

despairing will find nothing more or even a clue
why they even risked it as far as Little Rock
to eat from the sweat of another's brow

forsaking Georgia farms for Visa freedom
only to have an Ike send in the National Guard
for escorting integration up their high school steps

when soon enough franchises of Sears & Dillards
would pave another tempting parking lot
& issue disfranchising credit cards

till make it at last to the Mississippi
only to find it so low no barge can go
though Huck & Jim still raft & smoke

drift past each prejudice & deadly feud
unhurried on the same old undulant flow
the convict spent years in the shadow of

although unseen its subway rumble ever heard
bearing its constant flotsam of scum & twigs
whirling & seething at the Colonel's inherited banks

the scheming son's mansion tipped over & sunk
his seven lovely daughters swept away & under
by the rising waters of its unfathomable flood

for the Adelantado Hernando de Soto
a long wet kiss from his endless lover
as he sank a solitary sperm to her hog-sized fish

source of the false charity of a Con Man's plot
of those silent hosannas with their liquid theme
now in early June running unmajestic & thin

with snowfall low in the whole Midwest
spring come & gone with no trace of rain
& is it then an omen for all the loss

the little to be recovered on trekking back
to revisit the faded glory of a river's past
this Great Sire reduced to barely a trickle

its envisioned new freights & far other ends
its towering smokestacks all so grand
a royalty billowing balls of steam & soot

giant triple-decker wedding cakes
boilers overheating then bursting in flame
deadly holes blown in giant hulls then buried hulks

now poking up with drought their skeletons reveal
from Civil War the "Paul Jones" "Charm" & "Dot"
scuttled in retreat as archaeologists rope them off

in a race against Mother Nature swallowing again
scavengers sneaking around in search of gold
ripping off a relic the harness for mule or horse

a stack of dinnerware chipped & cracked
a bottle of antidote for ague or fever
a stern paddle hardly worth the wading

ankle-deep in slimy weeds
a crowd gathering nearby at Handy Park
where facing Beale Street W.C. stands a statue

with behind him & to the right
a ring encircles an urchin with a recorder in his mouth
three guitarists a trumpeter & a mechanical drummer

come to carry on a tradition of yellow dogs
of blind men singing on Depression corners
pilgrims to this Mecca to this training ground

for all-night sessions of the separate & unequaled
a Charlie Robinson discovering others' higher notes
were nothing to him his two octaves range enough

for reaching & holding any listener's heart & soul
who slugged corn whiskey & gambled till dawn
danced on the piano top to his own unrecorded song

grandsons & daughters tapping feet & clapping hands
keeping time as if this were where & what
the convoys & wagons were destined for

or was it Graceland & Elvis' grave
a gaudy show of bouquets & granite markers
photographs commemorating his patented shake

trim in his white suit red sash & Hawaiian lei
filmed on site in the Marquesas with palms asway
rowed between canoes on a banana-leaved stage

every native eye fixed on his slicked-back hair
though no more cannibalistic than moviegoers
would eat him alive in his B-rated scene

all still hunting him with chants of Elvis Lives!
as if by rearranging the letters of his given name
could bring him back who killed him with worshipped fame

their bloated King of Rock 'n' Roll
fallen to drugs & alcohol the price each paid
any for the treasured autograph or Snappy photo

for silk thread sequin or a single hair of his head
swooning as he crooned "Love Me Tender Love Me True"
oh something the dollar bills could never do

though to buy Golden Hits assured he would never die
his voice forever revived on "Blue Suede Shoes"
Death's cold iron bars escaped through "Jailhouse Rock"

staying with him at "Heartbreak Hotel" night after night
on the cover of *Life* his daughter his look-alike
brings back every feature down to his feminine lips

speaking in her first exclusive interview
of the pills he took of the gift he gave
her own battery-powered golf cart at the age of four

so was it worth it after all
if this is where the picture ends
or is it then that each may choose

even Lisa remembering a father's good
& this by choice once she's understood
the legendary man whose face her own returns

each city offering a Presley or a Father of the Blues
or others whose stories though lesser known
deserve retelling like that Mississippi moan

punctuated by Lunceford's flaming brass
anchored by Jock Carruthers on baritone
the Trio belting out those corny lyrics none surpass

"Muddy water in my shoes / I'm rockin' to the lowdown blues
I don't care it's muddy there / it's still my home
They live in ease & comfort there

I declare
my toes turn Dixieway
round & round the delta let me stay"

as much for the shoals & bars espied
as for such depths sounded in all they sang
their cargo of fellowship & sacrifice

those pulled together to make it up
when the current aimed to sweep them down
but this gets ahead of a tale began at Fisk

only later would Jimmie move to Memphis
here where two barbers attended the annual convention
in that first Faulkner novel had ever read

here the pair taking a decent room
wonderfully cheap though hardly getting a single wink
with noises all night through adjoining walls

people climbing stairs & walking the halls
squeaking springs with half-pained half-soothed tones
each evening finding on their bed or floor

or draped in the bath on tub or commode
ladies' intimate underclothes
couldn't figure it out & never would

& though this first night's accommodations
superior to any in a Modern Library edition
may yet remain as stumped as that couple of yokels

but plan to continue where the map will lead
to the eastern beginning of Estevan's Texas plot
retracing steps to a view from Mt. Everett's crest

next stop the Fugitives' gathering spot

2

in her 80s Granny Polk would always say
"I'm going to see my boyfriend in Nashville Tennessee"
but first she would have to fix her face

brush her dentures & do her nails
work herself into the girdle fasten snaps held up her hose
& step into a pair of her highest heels

at her home on Western Street near the country club
would prepare her same predictable meals
of celery sticks & black-eyed peas

mostly leftovers a dab of this a dab of that
a trait from Depression days when any scrap
left by boarders at breakfast she would always save

cutting crusts from the sandwiches she had packed
in black metal pails for those would find them
turned to bread pudding come suppertime

her birthday on Valentine's a dead giveaway
for her liking men & had them still on bended knees
she seated on a green bench in her beloved Saint Pete

at 15 had married Mose back in '98
grandad 10 years her senior & done for at 59
she said "the Oliphants die young"

the oldest child in her family sent at 13 to Murfreesboro
a country girl to care for a relative's brood of half-a-dozen
& forever swore "I'd rather be in jail with a broken back

than babysit a pack of kids" though even so
had six of her own the first two in Tennessee
the last four in Baird a junction just as barren as could ever be

but better for asthma grandaddy thought
yet would never evade his recurrent TB
to him his honey had hung the moon

& proud too of Fannie Lil Carl Doll & Winnie
though most of all of his Mosby Davis
the son to whom he gave both his southern names

died in '32 before his junior had gotten engaged
but had told his dad he had found his mate for life
even if had never talked to mom knew they would wed

heir to grandad's honest ways his mother's get-up & go
whose comic commentary on any lazy crew included her own
accused them of "laying with the dry cows all night long"

a good-for-nothing she called "a walking miscarriage"
lambasted herself as well for bearing them all
"I should have slept with my face to the wall"

after Mose retired would move to Fort Worth
she keeping cornbread & cabbage on the kitchen table
selling ready-to-wear as he coughed & faded away

with a powder puff she repainted her pink Oldsmobile
sent their elder son to A & M though it didn't take
saw the oldest marry an alcoholic with Hoerner box

mercifully grandad gone before he knew the worst
their first son ending his days in the State asylum
their first daughter's son in & out of prison

what would Mose have thought not dying so soon
living to witness the toll taken by their Texas move
leaving his "Athens of the South" for tumble weeds

traded Vanderbilt for a desolate railhead east of Abilene
or was it just from turning to him her tender face
that Brother ended up nutty a grandson shot cocaine

had met & married here where two decades later
Tate & Ransom taught & Lunceford took his college degree
did Mose suspect it "a nostril" through which the state

had long breathed the Northern air of free institutions
would he have ever imagined an ex-student's engines
set up in a Georgia Industrial School even amazed Klansmen

or when asked where he learned such mechanical skills
had answered they came of studying a bit of ancient Greek
did Mose & Polk believe it all just a coat of paint

scratch it beneath the surface & a savage would stir
or their brain suture's closing prematurely the cause
of higher faculties inactive after age twelve to fourteen

not wanting to think it yet must in recalling that past
in order as General Fisk said to learn "the terrible lessons"
a wonder dad never used the "N" word nor saw them as beasts

when out near Liberty one in a pick-up ran into him
he permitted that unlicensed driver to "pay as you can"
monthly like clockwork mailman delivered his five-dollar bill

dad's faith so like George White's who trusted still
when even Fisk his commander at Chancellorsville
turned down a loan for keeping open that failing school

& to think it would bear the General's name
White hearing the words of Leviticus 25 loud & clear
"the trumpet of the jubilee shall sound throughout the land"

with scarce food enough for one more week
this untrained music director would take on tour
his newly emancipated Jubilee choir

his singers deep in debt yet even so
out of proceeds from their recital in Ohio
donated to tragic victims of a Chicago fire

with no hotels willing to put them up
George would change their luck
instead of pop tunes had them sing their slavery songs

spirituals expressive of their American lives
at the White House for Grant sang "Go Down Moses"
to be greeted there with appreciative applause

sang in E-flat the "Battle Hymn of the Republic"
three half-steps higher & with no burnt-cork facial
in Europe the younger Strauss waving his violin

as the electrified audience threw handkerchiefs into the air
on hearing "He hath sounded forth the trumpet
. . . shall never call retreat"

Du Bois attended here then Harvard
where he found the teachers no better
said were only more widely known

& better paid though never so eager to feed
students hungered for a fruit so long forbidden
reading & writing such a holy mystery to them

starved more for learning than even for food
would sell scrap metal old rusty handcuffs
just to buy the power of talismanic books

while their teachers whipped & spat upon
pupils down Church Street on their way to class
openly stoned by the Klan in defiant parade

by World War I with 76 stars for Fiskites fallen
still the lynching & brutality would go right on
3,000 accepted a newspaper invitation to watch one burn

their music room in such sad repair
the wallpaper flapping in the winter's wind
& through the roof the rain pouring in

for an instructor's feet & lap only heated bricks
one would-be enrollee would write "I beg to state
that I wants to be come a student at Fisk

and wants to Board where I will be warm"
little knowing conditions so bad all women turned away
upperclassmen surviving summer on seven cents a day

& what became of White the pioneer whose troupe
Twain said he would walk seven miles to hear
even the Kaiser's men hoping to learn from them

when they brought to Germany their sorrow & yearning
their finest tenor spitting up blood with inspiring song
before that in Scotland his wife succumbing to typhoid

one singer always ill one suffered a stroke
as they poured out "Nobody Knows the Trouble I See"
the director himself prostrated with a hemorrhaging lung

& did Mose ever know of their Jubilee Hall
hear them sing "Steal Away" or "John Brown's Body"
would Tate's translation of Pindar have meant a thing to him

how could it to a switcher & shunter of freight cars
who likely had no suspicion any direct descendant
would know of or care to read "Blue Girls" of Ransom

or his "Bells" for John Whiteside's long-dead daughter
how could that assignment from Dr. Robert Nossen
have meant anything to him who just wanted to be certain

the westbound train was still on time
checking his pocket watch the one engraved
with initials now of four generations

his only heirloom he handed down
no message no signature just the registrar's
& doctor's on a standard certificate where

the Bureau of Vital Statistics recorded
principal cause coronary occlusion with
tuberculosis of kidney & lungs contributory

no autopsy performed no proof nothing to do but guess
he would not have had the least interest in any quatrain
with "word" & "sward" the fine off-rhyme

but why is it so important to know if an immigrant son
of some ignorant poor-white Scottish clan
born a Southerner in a defeated unreconstructed land

might have given the time of day
to Tate's "Ode on the Confederate Dead"
or bothered to agree with Lowell as to Allen's best

his marvelous "Swimmers" in terza rima
much less accepted indictment of lynching's strangest fruit
why even conceive a railroader could ever react

to his second son's coming to listen in fact
to Jimmie's two-beat swing with joy & love
when not even the Fugitives ever visited Fisk

to find & hear that future conductor's
Cotton Club Express
grandad's only line the Southern Pacific not one of Dante's

& yet there has to have been something way back here
to account for an offspring responding so deeply
each time he heard "Lunceford Special" & "Stratosphere"

or maybe owed it more to his mother's ear
she whose first name was Jimmie too
though her own taste ran exclusively to

saccharine sounds of that Champagne man
how ever explain how it came about
if not through blood how figure it out

maybe it's up ahead on another trail
one blazed by Boone or a Moses Austin
who said hundreds traveled not knowing for what

or whither except it was on to Kentucky

Ironing at the Colegio Mayor "Mara"

with a hiss of the steam
& a clank of the iron   bare-
footed winter to pennant race
she would press them all again
the short sleeve button-downs
& long sleeves soon outgrown

& while the hot slick metal
went sliding upon & smoothing
the sprinkled cloth   the radio on
to Dodgers fielding & batting around
once more she removed the wrinkles
with a proud & tender touch

then taught this menial task
to lazy brothers college-bound
would have   she said   no money
for cleaner's bills as did those frats
yet her younger pledged & back at home
brought his dirty whites with monograms

never minded not she no not at all
washed them summer spring & fall
so affectionate his way with her
so full of kidding & forever wore
his impish grin those years before
that fatal crash had carried him off

elder & yet less willing or able
to say how much it always meant
in imitation then half showed it
in humid Austin so long ago
a shirt for work each morning
& now here again in hot Madrid

following still in all her steps
collars first & then the yokes
backs fronts & between the buttons
the pockets & last each sleeve & cuff
a pattern for every memory of
her dressing sons with highest hopes

a belated poem to express
her steam iron's warm caress
its distillation of water poured
as she bent above that creaking board
to keep her boys handsome & clean
pulling for them as for her baseball team

Another Hill Country Sunset

while clouds pile up in puffs
like white-powdered coiffured wigs
in eighteenth-century drawing rooms

the sky imitates with its pinks & blues
a cheap religious painting
the sound system backgrounding with

the Young Cannibals' biggest hit
amplified for The Oasis' forty decks
built into its limestone cliffs

now look out & over a shining Lake Travis
where motorboats furrow the waters
while the crowd awaits the bell

will ring down the orange-pink ball
when all will pause from impressive talk
stop sucking on daiquiris or piña coladas

at tables with dips & tortilla chips
to applaud as it sinks below the hills
leaving its unearthly afterglow

know it because on occasion have shown
that sight to visitors from out of town
who have found it unforgettable

but personally prefer
to drive after supper
as far as the marina at Anderson Mill

to turn around & head unhurriedly back
by Libby's Dance Hall & the mysterious sign
reads among mesquite "Alma de mujer"

to cross the concrete bridge spans Cedar Creek
as it works its way around deep-bronze rocks
back of a spooky house for private parties

take the curves through a thickly wooded patch
of pecan & sycamore form a roof of leaves
cools in sweltering summers down twenty degrees

then climb to the open twilight
turn west on a road where off to the right
peacocks strut among goats & guineas

on the left a ranch with barbed-wire fence
where cattle by a live-oak stand
still graze against the fading light

chewing cuds & staring big-eyed
at a car pulls over & parks
a single longhorn looking up

moving slowly indifferently
knowing he's the one & only
though among the yucca & thistle in bloom

a barely visible doe will suddenly appear
first one fawn & then a pair
& then as if out of nowhere

through a thicket of brush & scrub
statue still in silhouette
an antlered buck will peer

the sky lit by a sliver of moon
then back up turn & aim the brights
where across the pasture headlights catch

their luminous eyes when then
even more will enter the meadow
while the heavens' herd glimmers above

Bert's Barbecue

once more have waited
till far too late
to list the credits due

pay respects to one has
made it all come back
as only now it dawns

on stepping in between
two sets of picnic benches
ten in all with space enough

for first one leg then the other
over the seat & underneath
this unpainted plank pine-wood table

with its knifed
names & initials
Amy + JD   Okie   Beto (of

Los Fairlanes could it be?)
Vs vibrating out from a
knot as if in shock

each built by him & his dad
& now for blocks around
the smoke from burning oak

scents this winter air
with chicken beef & ribs
has since 1970

at this alley
intersects with
MLK

after father Johnson
came from Scandinavia
settling first in New Sweden

then the family moving here to Austin
he a master carpenter
turned to barbecue to make a living

gone even longer than Bert
long before such friends as these
Tom Bob Ricardo & Don

have come for his famous food
for lunchtime talk of academics
to join with brokers

bricklayers programmers
secretaries plumbers
students & police

each group in its regular place
with filled cups & paper plates
as overhead Mickey rounds third base

to teammates' pats & handshakes
a homer along with trophy photos
antlered heads & horns of steers

here too on his in-laws' side
is grandfather Adams enshrined
in this city's softball Hall of Fame

while Bert in his bib apron
is pictured serving up
coleslaw brisket & beans

catering to *políticos*
like Lyndon Baines
attending too to Lady Bird

whose fruit trees & wildflowers
beautify Interstates & nature trails
she another Johnny Appleseed

while patrons here are more into
pouring on the Cajun sauce
sitting beneath a snapshot

of a prospector pans for gold
next to a wide-mouthed bass
a giant armadillo of papier-mâché

their hats & coats all hang on walls
on their welded railroad spikes
or hooks of horseshoe nails

while framed squaws bend over
blackened pots
stoking an outdoor fire

watched over by
Geronimo
armed & ready

next to a shot from a John Wayne film
another of a high-school football game
where Bert is driving his model A

from its rumble seat
white-gloved Sweethearts wave
& is shown too with Gus-ball lineups

or in his burnt-orange & white suspenders
standing all alone beside the rack
for Fritos & Lays potato chips

but features most of all for Texas fans
those moments from Royal's career
when Speyrer his speedy receiver

outraced a UCLA defender
outstretched still for hauling in
the winning pass or that epic scene

on Turkey Day against the Aggies
as Worster his wishbone back
plunges off tackle & barrels through

or that legendary season of '69
the Cotton Bowl vs. Notre Dame
4th down on the Irish 10

2:26 on the clock & behind by 3
the Coach with his headphones on
calling time to confer with Street

his quarterback whose surprising toss
caught them off guard & across the room
a facing frame of players leaping

arms signaling the score has brought it home
this tradition still carried on
by Joyce his wife of thirty-two years

Gary his son an avid sportsman too
who slices the fat
& chats of hunting

of pitches slow or fast

Vincent at the Wal-Mart Supercenter

the woman writing a check
for 45 dollars & 46 cents
the amount visible to all in line
in black against the eerie green
on the register's monitor screen
her hair beginning to thin
along the part in dyed red strands
have lost their sheen
her navy blazer gaping open
down the back where along the seam
its threads are working loose
has in her shopping cart
his Montmartre café scene
with a sticker reads five ninety-nine
the price of this matted print
slashed for a faster sale
more than he ever made
from rich shades & luxurious shapes
will now enliven her dull apartment wall
with his Paris night of flickering stars
above the sidewalk tables & chairs
romance at the extravagant cost
of that ear he razored off
quickly or did he slowly slice
to lessen or increase the pain
& whoever would
for the skies he daubed
his brush-stroked fields
his trees & swirling birds
have paid for those
with a pistol to the side of his head
or have squeezed the trigger
for this cityscape
she has piled in along with
shampoo & conditioner in one
snacks soft drinks & panty hose
surely he would have given it away
knowing how much she needs
to escape her advancing age
from her worn & fraying outfit
with a bank account if not overdrawn
can barely afford
the cheapest art

A Funeral in Brock Texas

the husband of a cousin had died
in boyhood lived next door to her
till moved away at the age of nine
felt obligated to go & pay respects
to attend another unctuous service
on the heavenly host & all the rest

went as much for his sake as hers
he a Native American quiet & kind
both so reticent were only together
through a blind date others arranged
eloped against her mother's wishes
their marriage lasting for fifty years

the church of a two-toned sandstone
erected in '39 the date engraved into
a V-shaped front above the entrance
where funeral-home man & woman
in black suits smiled Good morning
flowers at the altar with casket open

pianist & a handsome music minister
had begun with "How Great Thou Art"
his voice pleasant his notes controlled
seminary trained & had come to assist
their Baptist pastor who after the solo
said Let us pray as he bowed his head

afterwards asked for all to rise & join
in singing "Standing on the Promises"
following the hymn a review of his life
employed as a plumber but had studied
art in college & back from Korean war
had built their home of his own design

raised three kids & appointed deacon
a Christian in deed who lived religion
would rarely say a word but if he did
never against but always to encourage
the Reverend then urged his survivors
to carry on His servant's faithful ways

assuring his wife with a verse selected
from Nehemiah she would have a wall
support around her of family & friends
as well as members of their fellowship
should go on knowing his body a husk
left behind his soul gone to God above

at the cemetery his metal coffin draped
with stars & stripes graveside memorial
closed with "Amazing Grace" as slowly
undertakers folded the flag given to her
she received it with her habitual reserve
rituals expected not to accept or console

In Upstate New York a Texas Composer Has Lost His Home

his retreat & sunless escape became
his displaced music's needed landscape
of layered hills & quilted fields
marked off by maples in cold bare rows
angled to darkening clouds in crescendos
echoed by those lower in distant mist

while nearer the two-storey country house
(called Skåne after that ancestral province
of a grandfather wrote fine English prose
though by every other Swedish immigrant
kidded in Dekker for his heavy accent)
snow holds on out the porch's windows

facing east & west & south
to the winding downhill stone-
bordered shale-covered drive
& below it to a pond's ice-blinded
opaque pupil whose melted edges
mirror skeletal limbs & mobile sky

as leaf-littered banks contrast
with patches of muddied ground
or of greening mounds of grass
& a pair of lifting & falling willows
their thin branches a yellow writhing
against a stand of wet black trunks

squirrels racing out along their boughs
birds dipping or gliding in circles tighten
pheasant & deer now out of sight
have strutted brightly or bounded through
an unmown plot of frozen asters
plants nibbled until the garden fenced

took bankruptcy to keep this adopted scene
to set down its blustery overcast sound
would take as if by winter storm
the city's unavoidable concert halls
counter the noise & grime & ridicule
to earn too a return for arias in June

but in the end foreclosure has come
to evict the artist from his quiescent view
perhaps for the best in forcing him back
on memories of Dekker or a Newgulf youth
where despite inevitable loss with every gain
inspiration began & may again & will sustain

A Texas Version of Crèvecoeur

in the *Letters* of that eighteenth-
century farmer humans as plants
ingest their nature as inhabitants
of the air they happen to breathe

flourishing better on taking root
in soil untilled for earl or baron
a land they could call their own
transplanting to it Europe's fruit

as the Czechs had brought along
their names of towns back home
painted Praha's church the same
echoing too with liturgical song

but then with communities gone
to cities where the youth escape
their steeples now all rise alone
settlers at rest in nearby graves

forgotten unless a camera crew
revisit their sites for Public TV
to capture the intricate imagery
in sanctuaries the faithful knew

the State's granite capitol built
by stonemasons highly skilled
in their trade they carried over
from auld & bonny Edinburgh

freedmen erected the mansions
after southern-style plantations
laid track through eastern pine
swung blues boogie & ragtime

famous for rattlers & rednecks
a chili cook-off cattle & crude
yet also find any foreign food
distinctive dress local dialects

every city serves Thai cuisine
it's German *braten* in Gruene
in Nederland now Cajuns live
while Mexicans offer a votive

in their houses at Bolivar beach
the Mazzus Parigis Constanzas
like all Neapolitans love to fish
whose airs inspired opera arias

hear in the streets or recital hall
Buddhist wedding Bach gigues
as Chinese Japanese Taiwanese
achieve even in heat unpastoral

have witnessed return of buffalo
but not the roaming Karankawas
those replaced by a mix of races
African Arab & Indian on the go

accepting or rejecting new or old
poets like Konstantin Kuzminski
critics like Sudhakar Jamkhandi
enrich more than any black gold

& here in this yard in Cedar Park
a Chilean waters mountain laurel
blesses the native blooms & bark
as do Andes verses of her Mistral

from Teachers at South Park High

Aloline Pickell

her hands small with tiny fingers hung at ends
of short plump near doll-sized arms her wrists
with deep creases above which she would pull

her light-pink or her light-blue sweater sleeves
her narrow shoulders flaked by dandruff snow
never looked one in the eye just lids fluttering

as she sat at her desk in those high-heel slings
straps never staying up as handknitted sleeves
in grading taking off for leaning on the lectern

for ums & ahs & based presentation critiques
on Monroe five-step sequence from attention-
getter to need satisfaction visualization action

three favorites on forensic teams would sneak
her keys & instead of preparing their rebuttals
crawled out of stage's dressing-room window

as class continued drove her car from school
to a downtown beer joint to shoot some pool
returned & replaced her keys in purse as bell

sounded for end of period did she ever know
or did she just let them get away with murder
being more concerned with their enunciation

of arguments for or against could win debates
& trophies & be displayed in the awards case
do those make up for showing so little respect

Kathrine Bailey

on looking back it doesn't seem to mean a thing
yet its parenthetical numerals letters in brackets
two minuses make a plus equal a kind of swing

when at the end the answer to a problem checks
whether one likes reuniting broken bits depends
mostly on who conducts the class if all business

the way she was it can make a fateful difference
especially when humor is not added to the math
not being assigned the best & brightest students

as her colleague was made her resentful perhaps
honor society membership ended with the lower
grade from absences on debate & orchestra trips

of which she disapproved were among her sorer
points so took some off turning B to negative C
but for figuring it out requires a mind far more

adept than one can only solve for X dividing 3
by 5 or 6 placing a decimal on the proper side
multiplying numerators their equation the key

for explaining wholes of fractional parts decid-
ing if subtracting would give a greater amount
common complex compound still so mystified

by its being the basis of sound & can account
for every living thing except of course for her
who computed a number that really did count

Harold Meehan

was famous for his mercurial Irish moods
slamming down in disgust a stubby baton
on the stenciled music stand when woods

or strings missed his cue not coming in on
time but then on retuning a violin he'd tell
an anecdote a joke on himself the passion

subdued yet to rise again all knew so well
followed by the deep regret endeared him
at least to those placed him on a pedestal

for sounds he brought to life a Beethoven
1st Gershwin's Parisian horns Diz & Bird
buying the Rugolo *Adventures in Rhythm*

with school-system funds swing unheard
till he'd left his St. Louis home with Bop
in tow scatting notes spreading the word

of syncopation rehearsing for a sock-hop
Saturday night when stock arrangements
like "Jersey Bounce" a far cry from pop-

tune rock by a swiveling pelvis students
adored even with dance sinful in a Bible
Belt his job saved by the Superintendent

winked at his drinking did so for awhile
but at last had to fire him who on his sax
blew the young minds to jazz & classical

Alice Cashen

her honors classes reserved for talented types
not being one missed out on the inspiring fun
of her course in the fabrication of poetic lives

in that piney woods of a prosaic existence one
was living then & like all others giving the lie
to every prayer & profession of a regular Sun-

day attendance able only to glimpse her manly
walk with legs wide apart & somewhat bowed
with glasses hanging below her bosom held by

a chain or ribbon her hairdo not at all in vogue
her voice a little gruff but never heard it speak
of how to shape a story in an off-rhyme mode

recount a tale of boomtown life in a Sour Lake
Saratoga or her native Batson where she lived
& commuted from its scum once called a freak

of nature with bubbles flared & cured arthritis
drew a lawless crew of roustabouts & wildcat
speculators her '43 M.A. thesis on aeronautics

in secondary schools trained the air-age pilots
against the Nazi threat by means of a Pegasus
Icarus or Daedalus dream of da Vincian flight

learned if late its vocabulary of radio compass
de-icing diving physiological effects of flying
& from her camping essay its literary calculus

Revisiting the Scene

what a trip! to return to the time of resentment
acne puppy loves petty fears lessons forgotten
so many never learned when most were meant

to prepare & lead or steer one to or away from
naïveté not being aware of all there was to live
for with without or the much was still to come

to keep the mind & options open never to give
up on others or on oneself never less than one's
very best in any test trial or tribulation even if

no grade assigned or no award be granted once
the task is done the paper completed the course
finished when nothing's ever over only a dunce

would think a past will not catch up & reinforce
the rule & rebuke one thought to have left back
there with those believed so slow & dull hoarse

from repeating that same stupid insistent didac-
tic stuff about no plagiarizing taking good notes
staying up with the reading never being a slack-

er sage advice of course ignored on sowing oats
but oh! what fun to sneer & feel superior to each
& everyone or at the least those seemed the most

out of tune with a Hit Parade would always teach
more than their textbooks adopted by some dumb
committee no member of which dared eat a peach

Cedar vs. Live Oak

neither a law case
nor an athletic game
just a tall straight
trunk against a limb

which came first unclear
whether crooked horizontal oak
rubs furry upright cedar
or conversely—neither chokes

the other out—one
grows erect to reach
miraculous rays of sun
on other's differing leaves

green all year long
one flat broad ovate
the other with prongs
thin pungent pliable pinnate

unalike also in seeds
acorn counters pollen spore
makes the feverish sneeze
its adversary squirrels adore

though not really enemies
just competitors for photosynthesis
on the Hill Country's
hot dry limestone cliffs

preferring either opposes sense
summers need whatever shades
garden or flower-bed fence
requires sturdy enduring stakes

At the Farmers' Market

Saturday mornings by ten
someone rings the bell
for shopping to begin
when local farmers sell

produce out of pickups
spread tomatoes & elephant
garlics on table tops
offer native garden plants

the man from Moody
takes a customer's hand
& rubs it softly
with his special brand

of emu oil guaranteed
to cure cracked skin
other stands feature cheese
soy flan or German

beef but for kids
the big attraction is
the animals' circus tricks
begin in fifteen minutes

as the unicyclist balances
& plays his accordion
to announce the performances
including one by Lauren

Macaw his parti-colored parrot
perched on his shoulder
till every insistent tot
tugging at his mother

pulls her fingers towards
the ringmaster's makeshift tent
with its mongrel barks
of the amazing Chicken

Dog & Jumping Jack
will roll over dance
scratch imaginary fleas act
out parts Darren commands

who feeds them treats
after roles as pirate
or picnicker their feats
most pets can't imitate

but these distracted now
by the purebred passes
near when their trainer-clown
calls "time out" chases

them into his van
switches to a serious
illustration of the lesson
learned in a pre-calculus

class as he lifts
from the plastic bucket's
see-through blue-pink detergent-water mix
strings looped with suds

a breeze slowly inflates
as spheres seek mysterious
equation of greatest space
allowed volume to radius

then a yo-yo exhibition
lets the audience see
how an out-of-work mathematician
with a bachelor's degree

can walk the dog
& recreate the Eiffel
Tower leaves all agog
afterwards rocks the cradle

declares his mother overdid
it joking it's why
he's in this business
earns so little pay

but a teaching entertains
even the adult crowd
approves skills patience attains
proven by its loud

applause then next juggles
bowling pins while warns
pedestrians as he pedals
& beeps like horns

from honking backing trucks
& now finally brings
Lauren on whose trick's
counting by flapping wings

all love her stuff
but after another bite
he scolds her "enough's
enough bow good night"

& so in ending
gives his thank-you speech
& to kids bubble-blowing
kits one for each

March of the Penguins

a French film as objective
as the force of life itself
with its sad & splendid

as when at each year's end
emperors in separate gender
lines approach from opposite

compass points on returning
single file to mate again
at the exact same polar basin

the members of monogamous
pairs recognizing one another
from their remembered calls

lean their affectionate necks
& long beaks pointed upward
rubbing in graceful ballet

later the treacherous transfer
of mother's egg to
father's prehistoric feet

before it crack & freeze
while beneath the ice
seals ever swim in wait

for the famished female
will walk for seventy miles
in her short as if skirt-

hindered steps back to
the bountiful deadly sea
to replenish her gullet with

fish will feed their chick
if hatched beneath the male's
protective feather pouch

as he stands a convict shackled
by the delicate shell
he lifts on his cold-resistant

claw-like nails for over
sixty days with
no sustenance no relief

shuffling to seek at forty
below the sixty degrees above
comes from huddling among

his patient kind
as they gather against
the pitiless Antarctic wind

to preserve the species
in another of earth's
disturbing amazing displays

Of Burgers & Serpents

how ever have another Big Mac
with double patties & piggy fries
not because her doctor decided
to place his patient on a strict
low-fat low-cholesterol diet
but because her dear child died
from innocent rattlesnake bites

always on passing Golden Arches
or the registered BK sign
I think of that San Antonio mother
whose daughter played outside
on the plastic recreational slides
while her mother waited inside
for their fast food soon to arrive

then just before it was ready
she was there beside her mom
sobbing & saying my leg it hurt
where she asked then saw forever
purple bruises the mosquitoes made
believing so until the order came
& her darling girl lay quietly down

on his going out to inspect the set
the manager would find their nest
disturbed by her sweet little thing
o how after that could she ever get on
with the rest of her envenomed life
how ever go on eating or breathing
with those fang marks day & night

Ode to a '68 VW Bus

for Roger & Tom Funnell

high schoolers pedaling their bikes
& college students in their own or
their daddies' sporty late-model cars

give it in passing the V-fingered sign
as now symbolic it putt-putts along
through shaded neighborhood streets

have even seen a camper-style pictured
touring Chile's capital city with a living tree
growing right up through its cut-out roof

at the post office one man asked its year
wanted to know how much would I sell it for
said his daughter's MS had gotten worse

& to transport her & her batteried chair
he'd soon be needing a sliding door
like the dented one on this passenger side

would add a ramp he said but turned him down
how ever put a price on or tell its worth
having shifted it since bicentennial '76

steering it up & around the mountain curves
down through the Mexican tropics
valleys deluged by an August monsoon

through humid heat of vast Texas stretches
with their rolling or flat & monotonous plains
their thick pine forests & coastal beaches

had bought it used from an Arlington man
through his ad in the *Fort Worth Star-Telegram*
paid him just seven-fifty & have spent at least

four times as much on upkeep & overhauling
of its four-cylinder air-cooled engine
developed by Adolf's holocaust Nazi regime

though for those remember Woodstock Nixon
& Vietnam it mostly means the hippie movement
with its peace pot-smoking free-love communes

yet to our kids in the '80s just an embarrassment
shamed them so when its unpainted pink-patched
undercoat would appear outside their junior high

carried them & friends to rehearsals & concerts
one played bass fiddle another the cello
those their parents couldn't fit into fancy sedans

& when it came time for landscaping the yard
removed its middle seat for flowers & shrubs
shoveled in loam loaded up garden stones

till its hubcaps nearly touched the pavement
& how forget its serving as storage space until
could make room in the house for boxes of books

while the installment-plan still-unpaid-for
4-door lemon would fail to run
depended again on this poor old thing

so maligned by son & daughter who now
fight over who will inherit its rusted floor-
board its banged-up bumpers its flaking

roof its driver's side stained by
rotten eggs from a passing prankster
its latches unlocking

though it still rolls on
thanks to the mechanics
at Motormania

DeKalb: 14 February 2008

ten months after tragedy
had struck Virginia Tech
mental illness on Valentine's
took its toll again

here in Illinois heartland
where in geology class
the five student victims
were taking lecture notes

those have now returned
as did the ghost
of mobster Jimmy Clark
who haunted Al Capone

after his massacre on
love's only calendar day
begged it to go
& leave him alone

in his hotel room
while the innocent faces
pictured in this memorial
issue of NIU's alumni

magazine appear forever young
always hopeful ever aglow
in their ambered photos
despite insanity's senseless gun

had put an end
to dreamed-of college degrees
their dedication of lives
to each's chosen field

Bible-reading Gayle's cultural man
Catalina & Sergeant Julianna
teaching in elementary grades
athletic Daniel assisting with

applications for financial aid
& classical violinist Ryanne
counseling disturbed to avert
their taking random aim

Bad Day at Black Rock

drove with Wayne to the Gaylynn Theatre
for viewing in Cinemascope that '55 film
with André Previn's sinister score

the Southern Pacific whistling toward
a dry dusty place where not one train since '41
had stopped to take on or let off a single soul

not till McCreedy the one-armed vet
acted by Spencer Tracy comes to pay his respects
to a Japanese-American whose son had lost his life

in saving his fellow soldier's the role the actor plays
but the father already murdered by Pearl Harbor hatred
that & the water from a deep well Komoko dug

resented by Robert Ryan as Reno Smith
Ernest Borgnine in the part of the bully whipped
by McCreedy's cool one-handed jujitsu chop

a totally satisfying flick
then headed for a carhop drive-in
the Calder Avenue Pig Stand

for a root beer float
to celebrate that very first day
out without

an adult along
a big shot in the family car
looking for a place to park

not seeing until too late
a guy backed into that '52 Chevy
the policeman arriving

& conferring with that older man
who swore we had come
hot-rodding around the corner

as if in sitting still
we could have run into
& rammed his bumper with

the driver-side door he had dented in
the two men laughing together
thinking this kid's too young to drive

when to their total surprise
pulled out that brand-new license
yet given a ticket just the same

sent to the juvenile court to listen
to a delinquency lecture & after that
suspended from driving for three long months

by a judge whose daughter
all knew to be the high school punch
sweet on Wayne & his tennis-team friends

no Spencer there to set things straight
to turn that wrong into
a feel-good Hollywood scene

Driving Across the Llano Estacado

& right away the place names tell the tale
Lariat & Earth Sudan Bovina & Levelland
with ever the next-to-last bringing to mind
Stephen Crane's story his "The Blue Hotel"
whose Cowboy is stupefied to the very end
"bovine" the word that writer assigns to him

between Lubbock & New Mexico's state line
feedlots fill the air with their unbearable smell
clanging windmills pump the water by turbine
sprinklers on wheels irrigate the flattest fields
black liquid gold still drained by rusting wells
do such systems leave brains with lower yields

& make one unaware a partner cheated at cards
or do they place one in touch with the elemental
animal mineral four seasons hot cold mostly dry
rounds of plowing & planting crops so often fail
just passing through am amazed they'd even try
living off dust-blown pastures with cattle guards

its weather so unreliable a horizon ever receding
to the vanishing point or a heat-shimmering lake
a mirage reminds once more of how little comes
of it all with the same tasteless look-alike homes
lawns sun-bleached straw & musicians weeping
over mistreated women keep them wide awake

wonder why for this any would leave wherever
though many did & do today who love to wear
blue jeans & boots at offices same as at rodeos
to dance two-step to fiddles & whining guitars
underneath a sky lit up at night by myriad stars
birthplace of broncobuster another pigskin hero

just can't understand it & stay dumber than hell
cannot conceive of any choosing to end up here
even as the son of a father born & raised as near
as twenty miles east of Abilene & among his kin
spoke with this same accent have known so well
sooner or later as their needed rain it may sink in

Lone Star Stalag

> *after the book by*
> *Michael R. Waters &*
> *his students at Texas A & M*

captured in Tunisia in '43
the POWs made art instead of
lighting up Arabian skies with

anti-aircraft flak & in place of
following Panzer tracks in
desert sand mixed concrete to

cast a fountain shooting water
from the mouths of frogs
caught in a platter held by hands

of their sculpted kneeling nude
then cascaded into her cobbled
basin though only now in this

distant decade do photos reveal
her stunning face & another of
an unclothed statue six-foot high

since only rocks & basin remain
& a cement pedestal on which she
stood   nothing of the braid she

pulled above her breast her head
slightly tilted down in a meditative
pose as she contemplates what

we will never know
although it's clear through her
that her makers thought

of those so faraway
longed for their land recalled
by constructing castles   miniatures

complete with turrets & moats
with one flew a swastika flag
since some not all believed

Hitler in the end would win
one remembered his journey here
& engraved in his aluminum

standard-issue canteen
the scene of a veiled Muslim
with a water jug upon her head

followed by a turbaned man
both beneath a palm &
a gateway arch with a mosque nearby

& around its oval metal edge
listed the cities he had passed en route
Palermo Tunis Casablanca

Pittsburgh New York Philly
St. Louie & then
etched on the other side

the guard tower overlooking
their barracks & barbed-wire fence
& printed in all-cap letters

HEARNE TEXAS
U.S.A.
PRISONER OF WAR

while another drew himself
against the pointed twisted strands
with his number underneath

his eyes a dark resistant stare
another painting seascapes
one sculpted mortar ships

& a cross-legged man with on his
head a cowboy hat a hole in his
hand for holding his rod & reel

others erected a music shell
for performances by
their captive band

musicians once had played
under Wilhelm Furtwängler
works by Beethoven & Wagner

here led by Willi Mets
conductor in years before
of the Leipzig Philharmonic

a few staged operettas
sewing their own costumes
designing the sets themselves

delivering lines had learned
in remembered civilian days
while a few could not forget

their duty to the Fatherland
their loyalty to the Führer
& so with nails in sticks

battered to death
one among their own
they knew was not a Nazi

three escaped to discover
the vastness of the Lone Star state
its Brazos River too low to float

their raincoat-fashioned kayak
the trio welcomed at Christmas time
by a farm family invited them in

for dinner with all the trimmings
till caught by the sheriff's men
what moral to draw if any

for in every time & place
war & art have ever been
& though some men destroy

others seek creative joy
in any form
wherever they are

Elisa's Gift

she brought it in
for no special occasion
no reason really
other than the love
no father deserves

told me to close my eyes
I opened them
(closed so long)
to a roly-poly
doodle bug!

the best gift a guy could get
held it in my palm
touched its tummy
rolling it up in its tiny armor
defense against what on earth?

my own dad called me Dude
mother's name was Doodie
granny made it Doodie Bug
a doodler now
of gray poems pressed

in their soft-footed middles
ball right up
& roll away
would pen one to open me up
leave me so disarmed

as has this daughter's present
takes me back
to the knowing past
through a thing so small
yet sums & overwhelms

Donasio Checks the Mail

at not quite two
he's in no hurry
to fetch the cards
letters or brochures from

companies or persons mean
nothing to him names
he may have heard
but seen he cannot

read mostly goes for
stops along the way
to pick up leaves
elm oak sycamore in

distinctive shapes & shades
to him no news
compares with birds he
spots in neighbors' bare-limbed

trees thrilled more by
dog cat or bushy-tailed
squirrel than any dull
gas or electric bill

a winter catalog offers
super sales on gadgets
as yet he cannot
work or latest fashions

not one in his
own size but happily
delivers the pizza ads
to mom & dad

always eager to hold
to granddad's hand when
his sister turning four
prefers to stay at

home & play with
dolls or view her
videos & won't be
long till he too

finds it all a
bore bearing with a
slow old man has
nothing better to do

than hope for other
than another notice of
payment due acceptance instead
of standard rejection slip

though just watching his
response to our walk
brings tidings more timely
than stamped canceled envelopes

Amaya's "Dixie"

she works each day to
have it come out right
going over it once again
on this converted player piano
not knowing its history from

blackface minstrel to Civil War
just the tune & whenever
her fingers fail to hit
the correct keys & swing
its rhythm even Lincoln loved

its lyrics she perhaps has
heard but even if not
forgotten the land of picked
back-breaking cotton can hardly mean
a thing to her who's

never seen a boll or
a person pine to return
to the land where he/she
was born & there endured
indignity morning noon & night

she herself only concerned to
read & make the notes
on paper sheets sound happy
& free of any mistake
will gain her teacher's praise

Girl Gymnasts

for Annabella

before these pre-teens can cartwheel
& bend on the rail-like balance beam
handstand & scissor their lifted legs

do a split & after a double or triple flip
stick landings with steady heals & toes
they first must lift their arms & fingers

to ready themselves for tucking heads
on springing diving & curving torsos
only hands & feet touching the floor

& those precisely on the carpet's tape
of the same width as that narrow beam
preparatory to an artful athletic routine

but a higher act with distance between
the beam & surface of Wininger's gym
as now they practice on the level floor

bumping again their young little buns
on putting into action a phrase written
out on the entryway's dry-erase board

"Triumph is just 'umph' added to 'try'!!!"
aspiring not so much to ribbon or trophy
as to overcome all would keep them down

daring to defeat with bodies & minds
a fear of falling or of failing to perform
with a seeming ease & effortless grace

Boat House Grill

on Friday nights
it features "Yo
Gadjo" Slim Richey's

trio at its
family-style gravel-floored venue
with two holes

in its corrugated
roof live oaks
grow up through

while from its
ceiling hangs an
entire canoe &

near it a
fake netted trout
a real taxidermic

on the entrance
wall & on
its north a

trophy hung with
oars & life
preservers while on

a facing wooden
ledge outdoor motors
lean toward a

stage of planks
barely raised with
on it amps

mikes & the
instruments being tuned
for couples below

seated on green
picnic benches have
come to eat

to Western Swing
the food as
ever burgers catfish

& fries &
corn dogs for
all the kids

for the grown-ups
young & old
bock Shiner beers

they sip as
Django Porter in
his black-&-gray toboggan

begins to twang
Reinhardt's "Sweet 42"
his Gypsy namesake's

Hot Club piece
from World War
Two in tandem

with his leader
who's all decked
out in blue-jean

pants Hawaiian shirt
black white-banded hat
matching two-toned shoes

his white wispy
beard reaching not
quite down to

his palm-treed chest
as he strums
chords & peers

through his glitter-rimmed
women's glasses at
the shaking heads

& now on
all five strings
he rings out

"It Don't Mean
a Thing If
It Ain't Got

That Swing" then
follows it with
"There Will Never

Be Another You"
as Francie Meaux
Jeaux his barefoot

spouse keeps the
beat on upright
bass while letting

out a jubilant
yell as the
clientele pat their

feet on pebbles
from river bottom
or stream-fed lake

their children breaking
into delighted dance
until their parents

have them take
their grateful tips
& drop them

into the minnow
bucket of this
fisherman's music dream

Jazz by the Boulevard

for Donna Van Ness

yesterday
on a temporary
outdoor stage
the Heritage
named
for the Park Cities Bank
in recognition of & to honor
this festival's money-lending sponsor
Marchel Ivery performed at 69
& today on the Coors Light Main
David "Fathead" Newman at 74
is holding forth
Marchel having honked & swung on
"Star Eyes" "Bag's Groove" & "Lover Man"
now David doing the same in & on "Hard Times"
& also Hoagy's "Georgia on My Mind"
having opened with "Billie's Bounce"
as whites blacks yellows & browns of Cowtown's
crowd mill around or in portable seats
shake their heads & tap their feet
to the quartet's driving beat
out of reach of the shadow of Will Rogers' Coliseum
across from the Kimbell Art Museum
here for this "cowboy & culture" promotional scheme
a city manager's dream
to celebrate the Lone Star's native sons
to generate a few jobs & a bit of income
for local citizens the majority in shorts
& most everyone sports
a pair of shades from the sun's late September blaze
as even in these autumn days
it just keeps burning on
bright & unseasonably strong
with a little of the force
of these Texas tenors
blowing yet with might & main
despite age's unrelenting aches & pains
rhythm-a-ning or improvising a blues
or on pop tunes of Tin Pan Jews

bring joy to all have come to hear
who never knew a Ku Klux fear
here one block over from Camp Bowie
brick-paved Boulevard intersects with University
where admission is gratis
thanks to Cadillac's
major financial grant & to volunteers
manning booths including that Rocky Mountain beer's
causes one to wonder does hurt & happiness accord
with the roots of a minor chord
can the melodic blend in any song
set right a lingering wrong
it seems so to go by the loving-it look
when these Black men cook
with their hard-bop licks
their soulful stratospherics
a look apparent on every listener's face
regardless of race
or place of birth
due in part to an elegant auto's corporate worth
but most to elder statesmen hanging on
to produce a dateless priceless tone

Rondo for Mahler

one hundred years
from the time
he penned his

Ninth one hundred
five from the
date of his

Sixth have tried
to imagine him
coming back though

in spite of
Gospels & Hamlet's
ghost whoever has

yet wonder what
he would have
made of compact

discs render his
nine & unfinished
Tenth his own

versions will never
hear except for
recordings of him

performing pianola transcriptions
of his Fourth's
finale & from

the Fifth his
own first movement's
four-note fateful knock

Beethoven's famed tattoo
Gustav changed to
the one same

trumpet pitch until
with the second
time it returns

instead of down
the phrase's final
note goes gloriously

up & so
depend for his
orchestral sound on

conductors such as
Mengelberg who knew
him then whom

William Carlos Williams
in *In the
American Grain* likens

to mother Lincoln
in beard top
hat & woman's

shawl hovering over
his nation torn
by Civil War

coaxing from aching
instruments tumultuous loads
though Willem's Adagietto's

perhaps too saccharine
for its redemption
the composer meant

by his manic
transcendent theme how
many stars now

would that maestro
receive from the
Amazon reviewers rate

the latest CDs
with Gustav's understudy
Bruno Walter's "Resurrection"

& Claudio Abbado's
Seventh earning five
though Sony has

yet to reissue
the former's wondrous
Ninth to bring

back from '55
Eduard Flipse's Rotterdam
Sixth maybe out

of print since
Mitchell graded it
"aspiring but mediocre"

o how it
hurt to learn
of that critic's

cutting critique of
that very LP
on which first

heard its Andante
with his ardent
Alma 6th her

interval a "longing
languishing leap" followed
by its anguishing

minor turn captures
her though considered
by some "more

sob than song"
those asserting it
disturbs & makes

trivial the classical
form others so
certain he took

no pleasure in
its torturous melodic
line & yet

when he played
it for her
they wept together

his cantabile love
in returning again
has moved to

this centennial review
of the notices
& unkind cuts

include those accuse
Bernstein of directing
overindulgent emotional shows

when he it
was in part
recovered the symphonist's

art after the
Reich defeated &
ovens opened though

long before its
Holocaust Gustav gone
who knew well

Wagner's Aryan supermen
even before advent
of phonograph &

film could have
saved & replayed
his grail baton

his magic wand
in conducting of
his Seventh's sentimental

ironic parodic tangle
of lugubrious ländler
& misty cow-belled

nocturne how to
tell which recordings
to choose of

which he would
have approved when
Simon Rattle's Tenth

receives 3½ the
Third of Jesús
López-Cobos & James

Conlon's Fifth awarded
5 can Olson's
Black Mountain Projectivism

light the trail
through cold hell
& selva oscura

as do the
winds & strings
through "harmonic thicket"

"to pastoral tone"
or is it
all "a dreadful

farce" as Christensen
stated predating Hopkins'
essay in the

Barham *Perspectives* volume
his piece on
form in the

turning-point Fifth opens
with its "torment
of uncertainty" its

"becoming" requires "one
perception lead quickly
to the next

until all are
exhausted" & true
as well for

listener & conductor
as Mitchell declares
(with likely Flipse's

Sixth in mind):
"to survive the
length of the

symphony's finale alone
one needs a
musical constitution of

almost unnatural strength"
& goes too
for working one's

way through Jonathan
Williams's *Jubilant Thicket*
with its poem

on each symphonic
section who for
the Third's 2nd

movement drew upon
its "What the
Flowers in the

Meadow Tell Me"
selecting naturally for
the Fifth's rondo

a nature thought
from Thoreau's June
journal taking from

Schoenberg how he
had gained more
watching Gustav knot

his tie than
bigwigs treating sacred
subjects & were

Gustav to return
would he even
be surprised to

find Ives (who
in one Jonathan
limerick gives hives

to those hear
his recycled hymns)
with more than

one CD for
each of the
Connecticut Yankee's symphonies

since had the
Austrian lived had
planned to conduct

Charles's Third anointing
him America's greatest
composer carried its

score home with
him to his
early death in

his land struggled
to come to
terms with his

expressive Bohemian mode
those sort of
Mitchell's words in

Walter's "Vienna a
musical battlefield" where
citizens fought over

the arts with
impassioned partisanship while
Gustav's own tempestuous

temperament loosed storms
about his head
fisticuffs at the

first performance of
his innocent Fourth
his excesses still

in '57 arousing
hostile reactions &
yet he knew

his time would
come by '60
catalogs offering 5

competing readings of
the First 2
of Second 3

of Fourth &
2 of the
Ninth the Sixth

with a single
disc Flipse's if
"aspiring but mediocre"

inspiring nonetheless as
is Abaddo's of
the Seventh's strains

"native to the
night" even if
an ear-trained friend

knows far more
judges the whole
"a big disjointed

bunch of episodes
the Finale just
will never work"

the same magnificent
soaring rondo how
ever be brought

to agree can
any two yet
do with Mitchell's

nothing kills his
music like the
cozy approach smoothing

over soft-pedaling rather
than exposing his
noisy march thumb-to-nose

will ever accept
his intractable uncivil
double-faced moods his

nocturnes recurring not
trite but fighting
to unfold with

"unnatural strength" with
linked dynamic extremes
guide one Virgil-like

through brambles dense
with conflicting chords
in himself &

in responsive souls
as he waltzes
all through darkest

woods of macabre
scherzos to the
adagios of luminous

pulse wring the
heart with a
delicious pain would

endure again &
again a suffering
never repeated enough

from *Memories of Texas Towns & Cities*

Woodville

my alpha & omega brought it back
on wanting her china shelf moved
& to make it fit on the facing wall
had needed to saw six inches off

from the yellow pine with its rich
aromatic history ring after ring
wondered what year its trees cut down
was three since her garage-sale find

from one before the Great War's start
Stravinsky arrived through the FM set
with rumbling timpani & slashing brass
a thunder accompanied the serrated blade

as it ripped & tore into & through
all four seasons with their sun & rain
soaked by the rhythmic rise & fall
of that composer's primitive strains

on conducting then at the kitchen sink
a dance of adoration   a ritual letting
with dust piling on the linoleum floor
spilling as if that virgin's blood

in innocence to pool once more
with its pungent sap pulsing again
sticky & smelling of fictive boards
the Joe Christmas mill in August light

in what ground did the roots go down
under what sky did the needles grow
did they share that past of Scouting days
or further back when Wood had fought

Creek & Seminole in that shameful defeat
later at Galveston Bay with his wife kids &
30 slaves   afterwards a hero at Monterrey
elected 2nd governor of this Lone Star State

Allan Shivers held the post longest of all
here his house still brings the tourists in
to the museum the tour guide recommends
allow half an hour attend the Dogwood Fest

come when the tree's in bloom & hear its lore
how it served for a cross crucified the Lord
blasted by God Almighty so twisted & bent
none could think it meant for lumber again

its red berries standing for oozing drops
from rusty nails leaving brownish prints
on the tips of white blossoms' petal skin
or were they growing in the 1950s when

had chopped up logs for the council seating
at Camp Urland near Wood's namesake town
off the highway & reached by a red clay road
passing by Chief Drive-In's corrugated fence

led to the wooden arch of the Camp entrance
to its fallen pine cones & its sweetgum leaves
where she whose wish is a warm command
sent her gabbler to revisit that defining scene

when that summer job as a junior assistant
brought reveille earlier than for all the rest
those taking on slowly their handsome tans
instructors of rowing canoeing & rifle range

while with morning noon & evening meals
sorted the silverware stacked the dirty plates
cleaned again the peanut butter & jelly jars
swept mopped & scrubbed the dining hall

sweated from steaming dishwashing machines
lost at night at poker till the others sneaked off
to neck with their dates cabined across the lake
or those from town drove their daddies' cars

cooking outdoors had earned in years before
a merit badge with black kettle stitched in cloth
but recall more that patch could never sew on
would have permitted a learning of secret codes

chants with feathered headdresses & tribal beads
all because even though was one of a chosen few
tapped out & hung with a prickly holly wreath
had broken Order-of-the-Arrow's silence rule

but first blindfolded & scratched by undergrowth
left to sleep the night alone   no cot   no bedroll
just two matches & told Build a fire in the morning
Burn the wreath   If not the boot   yet made it through

then warned From now on not a word till six at night
assigned to saw up trunks & hack the branches off
the guy in charge the one OA in that Trinity troop
& was not about to give any rival half a chance

while other tap-outs were granted one & even two
on letting a phrase slip without their meaning to
with him   not on your life   asked a fellow scout
if he'd mind passing an axe   got it okay   & good

yelled That's it for you   Report to the mess hall
found the Master over coffee in that gloomy room
confessed Yes have a big mouth Can't keep it shut
Most every time have opened it have tasted foot

& happened again   when all she wanted was
her shelf cut down & moved to the opposite wall
not running it off with tales from the Piney Woods
jabbering on of ballet or a battle won at such a loss

San Antonio

"Every Traveler Needs a Mission"
the clever *Texas Monthly* tour guide reads
then lists & pictures each in turn
& Concepción as it should be first in line
followed by the other saintly three

San José   San Juan Capistrano
San Francisco de la Espada   the last the only one
have never seen   each a church from 1720 or '31
all built by tribes could only receive
their land & water from the Spanish king

masses still held for those who live nearby
though friars & soldiers gone long long ago
who prayed under beams of Rosa's Window
or quartered close to the fortress gate
to protect against marauding Comanche raids

was driven here first in summer dark
from Fort Worth in '44 to find & see Dad off
fed up with bombers on the graveyard shift
he had up & quit & though with wife & kids
was subject still to the wartime draft

stretched out in the backseat half-asleep
frightened by shadows cast in Forest Park
its limbs of trees at midnight black & tall
while another soldier's wife drove the car
heard vaguely mother's talk of daddy's call

then awoke to Brackenridge Zoo's animal stink
to husbands stationed at Fort Sam Houston
had made it together through basic training
find now it is never done   each week again
this marriage for twenty years rebegun

from the day María's mother held back her tears
holding to one another for reasons half-understood
clearer here on this second honeymoon cannot afford
in a room taken at this cheapest of motel chains
its brown-&-orange bedspread coast-to-coast the same

now hold each other closer knowing it more than fate
the kids left with their Texas granny who lives alone
traveled all night to arrive before he would leave next day
being transferred out to Fort Belvoir   gone perhaps
forever   how ever take leave of María   what did he say

barely recall that time at all   his return much more
envied on getting out of class to meet his train
how it moved so slowly   then let off steam
the platform lined with trunks & duffel bags
red caps loading footlockers into yellow cabs

spittooned waiting room where benches filled & emptied
with families would let out screams then hug & kiss
though on his stepping down from a chalk-numbered car
mother swore to him she never would
not until he shaved that ugly moustache off

& while she carried on & turned her face away
felt his uniform's stiff pant leg
rubbed his winter overcoat of heavy wool
spotted the insignia of his engineering corps
eager to know him & hear how he won the war

too young then to take it all in
& later would fail to seek him out
to learn what it meant to drill with men
were soon to die or thought they might
in army issues & haircuts all alike

in wonder watched him lather his upper lip
as he first told a story he would tell for years
of his whole outfit being shipped overseas
except for him who had happened to look around
for another type of work than policing grounds

not to pull latrine or mess-hall duty
something more in his printer's line
found an office with a shop behind
volunteered to sweep & pick up trash
then stopped his broom & sneaked out back

cranked up a four-color none could run
outranked but suddenly in big demand
attached to their unit & assigned to teach
the printing of strategic maps for Uncle Sam
while now fingers search a sweeter terrain

reach from head to foot while mouths explore
renew old landscapes with each touching press
of embrace's ink   blushes at such sensual talk
a coyness according with her simple dress
becoming to an ample mind cannot read enough

in the light covers up & never shows off
so hurt by her pushing of this hand away
from the one at times has caused deep pain
taken wrongly as a sign her love had waned
who has proven it true again & again

Stephen Crane: its hills & valleys they came upon
out of the sea their white & golden banner of Spain
Indians mere dots of black on the vast Texas plain
saw a moving glitter of silver soldiers   the long
battle of those & of priests against barbaric hordes

polished their armor with neatness & skill
at dusk their yellow stone towers calling with bells
ruins now besieged by indomitable mesquite
summoned to her through an interview conducted here
on a front porch by the Superintendent of Hebbronville

from there set off on the Mission Trail
would lead to Santiago & down the aisle
the favorite motif of this Chilean muse
who planned this visit to Concepción
where the Reverend Francisco Aponte y Lis

who before his death at ninety-three cured chiggers
with olive oil applied at room temperature
whose well nor her inspiration has ever run dry
from the very first unworthy of such & so unearned
other than she only the Service took any interest in

a body & mind so awkward so immature
though on turning twenty-one pre-inducted the same
bused here for testing & made to stay the night
on an upper bunkbed's mattress sagging & stained
then examined next day & declared 1-A

though in the end to escape induction
when among so many had gone unnoticed
how not by her   tried to enlist but was underweight
brought that fact to attention of Sergeant in charge
let go without a dime ninety miles from home

as Dad too had eluded the clutches
of active duty & the line of fire
wonder did he feel as guilty
when others fell in the vineyards of France
as in the rice paddies patrolled in Vietnam

or did he side in his unread mind
with the likes of the Alamo's Moses Rose
he a Bartleby type who preferred not to fight
despite Colonel Travis's heroic plan
for holding out to the very last man

to make like a porcupine huge & terrible
to be swallowed by the Mexican god of war
Bonham twice going out for reinforcements
his cream-colored horse shot from under him
but returned both times to face the inevitable

Rose a dogged philosopher of inverted courage
whose sudden refusal came in the face
of a bravery as ever considered supreme
climbed the wall & looked back down on all the rest
leaped & lit out for the wilderness

to run rather his butcher shop till '42
then in '50 to cross the Cajun border
& meet in Louisiana his natural death
while Dad regretted he had not stayed in
said he could have retired after twenty years

lucky for these in platooning with her
each reconnaissance a chance to zero in
on a topography whose strategic target
is this lone outpost of mutual defense
with sacrifice offered at no command

differences remaining unsettled still
opposites in any barracks on equal terms
daily retrained as the rawest recruits
each rough & bearded caress surrendered to
unconditionally accepted by her soft & smooth

Salado

a tourist stop lives
off what it was
long before the race of man

found its unspoiled creek
written up in the travel guides
& illustrated with color photographs

a glamorizing of historical facts
how stagecoach line & Chisholm trail
ran right through its scenic view

dusty teams & cattle splashed in
the stream cleared & cleaned itself
still offering now nostalgia for

its magic flow
the image of buffalo wading in
drawn here before

the tribes in turn would be
camping beside its banks
then followed later by

Spain's explorers gave the name
with its oak shade ever inviting
its watercress growing the same

picked mornings by a Mexican pair
before the crowds drift in
among the knickknack gifts

& so have come
to its roadside inn
to spend the night

to escape the kids
& what's routine
already missed after

a day of sights
of houses built
in Greek revival style

slave quarters
& other haunts
transoms porticoes & weathervanes

of this "Athens of the South"
with its literary society Texas' first
today the site of its "think tank"

hosts the deepest minds
seek solutions to war & death
brought on by the worst & best

greets a gathering of Scottish clans
& since each needs some group
to belong or to come back to

cannot resist
Bluebonnets & Thistles
a shop run by a man & wife

he of Scots descent
she   he says
part Cherokee

specialize in kilts & tartan cloths
discover in their official catalog
the pattern called Black Watch

then long once more
for its inherited unknown world
wonder how & why they showed up here

at this very spot
while in other shops
see teddy bears & patchwork quilts

antique glass & pewter ware
María drawn to
a sawed-out cow

with its bag & teats
all fixed to a platform with
underneath it a roller set

though lacks one leather ear
need it like another hole in the head
yet buy it nevertheless

hoping perhaps to half-hear
the squish-squish
of a superior day

ask the man who tends
the Double Eagle Hardware
what on earth

are the roosters for
the ones cut out from tin
then hear him say

"it's only what you see
something else to sell
like the nails in that barrel"

one room filled
with posters of early Fords
Chevrolets & Packards

glass tops from pump machines
for Gulf & Texaco gasolines
cleanser ads with Gold Dust twins

racism's grim reminders
though scoured will never fade
& yet for most has meant

a slower easier way
with its records kept in
the Central Texas Area Museum

though find it closed
no hours posted anywhere
other eager vacationers

with cupped hands
peering in
through grimy window panes

intent on catching a glimpse
of that distant simpler time
ask the lady across Main Street

when will it open up
hear her say "let me know if & when
you ever find Lucille is in

but I wouldn't get
my hopes up none
if you never see it

you won't be missing much
it's like this shop of mine"
with its live oak growing

in one wall
& out the roof
"I keep it open nine to five

but any time I try to close
people just can't stand
not to see what's here inside

as you can tell
it's not worth writing home about
hardly any that come on in

buy a thing
but still they have to have
their 'look around'"

what all can find
in summer's heat
are shade & water

enough to cool & quench
although will still be thirsting
for that life have left behind

& for the one will never lead
unless it's through the tasting of
an old-time native recipe

nothing real's for sale
& come right down to it
who would make the trade

Paris

have never traveled to see the Eiffel Tower
nor felt the need to view Wim Wenders' film
as a graduating senior only walked in the sewer
hiding in the dark & dank with Jean Valjean

when Mrs. Test-on-the-First-Line-Skip-a-Line
gave no partial credit for half those pages never end
none at all unless read Hugo's whole *misérable* thing
though after high school got through it just the same

came in fact not to want to put it down
wouldn't think to either this Texas town
dreamed of while in exile in Sooner land
where the drinking water could never stand

envisioned this as some green & exotic place
supplied in summer sacred colas half-frozen
its magic name felt on their see-through glass
on the bottoms of bottles saved for cashing in

returned the way those Texas memories always did
when every Saturday earned a dollar to spare
from the prescriptions biked or cotton picked
The Daily Oklahoman peddled on that Altus square

whether true or false non-fiction or carpet ride
each swallow not so much a secret formula with fizz
as the journey back to origins & native pride
a taste of what it was to thirst for & forever miss

Johnson City

at the boyhood home
of Lyndon Baines
wisteria reaches out
wanders & twines

crape myrtles stand
like giraffes in bloom
their splotched
albino skins

stuck with dried
cicada shells
dropping them when
the parchment curls &

falls away
live oaks with
their limbs lopped off
to delay arthritic bends

the peach a miniature
bears the heat
till its fruit is left
sun-ripened red

mimosa hackberry
magnolia cedar
all branching here within
a barb-less fence

while inside the house
his forensic text
lies open still
in the living room where

he learned to speak
of how to shed
to outgrow
& then live on

to save the past in
a city block
then imbibe it as
rural light & water

can turn to sweetest sap
to advance   to move on up
to fly worldwide
in Air Force One

to review the troops
the missing in action
or those with arms & legs
lost to grenades or mines

though not so far
nor for so long a time
that a Chief-Executive cattleman
can't climb back in

a Hill Country saddle
& ride the coastal Bermuda
to a ranch-style brand
of gelding humor

then attend
a Saturday afternoon barbecue
or to visit strength-
renewing settlers' graves

said the best manure
for any land is
its owner's own
familiar step

& though that tall
drawling leader's gone
his grasses still green up
to fatten beeves

& barring a
late spring frost
orchards promise
a record crop

all these husbandry brings
agree or disagree with
the campaign rooted
in rhetorical dirt

from Fort Worth: The Bathroom

for Aunt Sis & Uncle Alvin

for years would come here
on business & pleasure
to the source of words
you would never use once
& when any mouth had dared to
you washed it out with soap & water

latching both these doors to bedrooms
would keep the unzipped cousins
from getting caught by the pigtailed sort
they from being surprised naked as jays
whose differences still thrill to this day
not alone of the glorious enigma of sex
but of others after being let in on them
by love & a wedding in a Chilean church
& by the making & raising of one of each

to open these two doors discloses now
the many scenes & senses return once more
from when ran through them & circled around
from the front bedroom to middle & third in back
then into the kitchen where with popcorn listened
as the Inner Sanctum cracked its creaking door
long before an end to the war-&-peace decades
of your saving to fix it up   & though you did
it remains the same   at least recalled from then

where out this uncurtained window can see again
the cottonwood's seeds drifting down as snow
its trunk as big around as a hogshead barrel
cut down after a fallen limb damaged the roof
when you found its insides hollowed smooth
from woodpeckers living & eating within
as we spent vacations with visiting kin
& you worked on it little by little
as it has on this memory forever since

the oval mirror in your antique frame
still awaited in the attic for being hung here
for giving back the reflections of faces & hair
above the new tiles & the widened washbasin

would replace the old ones chipped & rusting
crowded about for scrubbing combing brushing
water pistols loaded for shooting through screens
boats powered by candle or a wound rubber band
stocked at times with tadpoles crawdads or goldfish

before the linoleum got ripped up for good
its patterns of dots & colored designs
grew faded & formed such mysterious shapes
had seemed like galaxies of stars & planets
or maps in an atlas with countries unnamed
unfound in astronomy or geography text
all worn from splashing & scuffing the floor
from those dashings in & out & back & forth
when you both yelled "Don't bang that door"

the wallpaper had known a far better day
yet never to all your nephews & nieces
who made out in stains the brown-edged faces
friendly at noon   so frightening by night
with its bare boards & nail heads peeking through
squinted at with bedtime on the bathing of feet
trying to decipher the signals or messages sent
yet covered by masks of gauze-like webbing
kept ever uncertain   kept forever guessing

the doubled-over lip of the white iron tub
had shown its age   that its hour had come
though filled with youth   its ships & coffers
to a spilling over from plunging beneath
for treasures sunken to its sandy bottom
& while its spigots with unmatching handles
the broken for cold   the enameled for hot
dripped their last as ticks of a clock
they yet poured forth a liquid of timeless relief

the new commode would have no brick
in its sweat-lined tank   the reason unclear
perhaps to float the bulb like a big copper bud
by raising the water level to the cut-off quicker
unstoppered its insistence running on & on
with a tone the adults couldn't stand to hear
its singing to them such a monotonous whine
but with that heaviness there at its heart
how could it have hoped to flower instead

were ever reassured by the aroma of linen dried
outside in Tuesday light   if rainy   inside
on a collapsible wooden rack   patched & folded
then stacked in the closets would never shut right
ever leaked a freshness of your laundered towels
rinsed & pulled through a hand-cranked wringer
rubbed on a tin rippled board   the whites blued
from a bottle with on its red-&-black label
a funny prim matron with her hair in a bun

now shiver to glance at the ivy outside
darkens the ground around hole-pitted slabs
a rock-paved walk between the houses & yards
Granny's across the way   its chimney & shrubs
its unlit living & dining rooms she wandered alone
cursing Granddaddy after he had left her at last
unable to endure longer her nagging complaints
moved to Meridian Mississippi & a widow there
would watch with him his beloved minor league

had bought Granny's house not letting her know
a copy of the one in Dallas she simply loathed
from its site downtown towed it here next door
"plum out of town & nearly in the country"
the maid grumbled who worked awhile for Granny
this house he sold to his stepdaughter & son-in-law
who the year of Wall Street's fall first made it home
their fiftieth now recalling all the relatives reared
uplifting histories would hear winter to autumn

not of Machine Gun Kelly holed up in Cowtown in '33
whose first sub had come from a local pawn shop
robber & kidnapper unwanted either dead or alive
would rather capture you gardening or mowing the lawn
your holding up through wetters of wallpaper & beds
those who failed after flushing to jiggle the handle
your footing the bill for ice cream cranked by hand
for cooling off in August from a hundred degrees
as you planned to remodel & refurbish this room

to most your city has meant a radio show
with Bob Wills & the Doughboys fiddling to sell
Light Crust Flour & Pappy's gubernatorial bid
but for some that music has never appealed
not so much as sights & sounds return from here
this unmentionable place with its unspeakable poem

The Cowtown Circle

*for/after exhibit curators
Scott Barker Jane Myers
Ronald Watson   Mark L.
Smith & Stephen Pinson*

their art back then still lay ahead
but even in War was being made
though unsuspected then & only
come upon at a '92 exhibition in

the Huntington Gallery long after
had built from Uncle Alvin's Vic-
tory garden those corn-stalk forts
no defense against an Axis attack

just played like after the Saturday
matinees at the White Theater on
Hemphill Street in this city where
the West began as an outpost pro-

tecting from the real not those pic-
tured redskin raids yet even by '39
Bror Utter declaring in a manifesto
bluebonnets & Indian paintbrushes

cattle auctions & rodeos all old hat
he & other Circle artists inspired in-
stead by the imported Parisian style
of abstraction myth & masquerades

in fourth grade aspired to cowboy-
Indian sketches of classmate drew
if knew Amon Carter collection of
Remington oils & Russell-sculpted

broncobusters do not recall but did
watch as bulls spilled riders at Will
Rogers Coliseum memorial to trick
witty roper statued on horse's back

outside in actual cactus as clowns
inside distracted till safe & sound
& at Forest Park saw a giraffe not
Veronica Helfensteller's from '43

sits at a table with mandrill & girl
her tea party for the social baboon
nor later '46's *Animals at the Zoo*
includes it may be a baby alligator

not so gruesome as when with full-
sized frightful teeth & armored tail
one rose from the lily pads to fasci-
nate in its rock-lined pond that last

to visit Sundays when the engineer
on miniature train blew his whistle
evokes their "intimate modernism"
so transfigures this formative place

as in her '47's *Poor Little Girl Who
Swallowed the Seeds* where its pair
of giraffes is staring down as vines
grow out of nostrils & into her ears

a cat curled up at her thin bare foot
& it could be a greyhound she pets
back then only read to that story of
bean stalks climbed to giant's gold

never knew then nor there nor any-
thing anywhere like her plates she
etched & yet did pass on a city bus
to Downtown "Y" that St. Ignatius

though would not have recognized
from her '43 *The Three Guardians*
its Victorian-era Academy still ex-
ists but without those spooky trees

& two white foreground female fig-
ures like floating ghosts glide back
of its low black wrought-iron fence
as a third stands on a 3rd-floor roof

arms as if ready to fly into a stormy
moonlit sky or to dive onto the leaf-
strewn ground below & as to *Three
Virgins Three Giraffes & Turtle* can

only make out in her plate from '45
two of her jigsaw-puzzled creatures
facing opposite ways while one hat-
less virgin turns & exchanges looks

with on the right that tallest living
quadruped the other virgins sport-
ing feathered hats peering straight
ahead at three pears on a table one

per plate while her turtle stretches
its neck to gaze up from the beach
or bank at pair of pears on another
plate & beside it a bunch of grapes

her alter-ego also featured in '47's
The House that Jack Built alone in-
side with a single bird flies outside
no dog cat rat cock cow horse as in

Mother Goose accumulative rhyme
any print run small from a wartime
shortage of paper & lead & so Dad
had to close their Standard Printing

at 1404 Throckmorton since bigger
outfits had hoarded needed supplies
then to work on Vultee's nightshifts
riveting B-24 Flying Coffins & part-

time at elder Utter's lithograph firm
his son in rinsing with collodion the
large glass plates & learning a trade
later to produce his '41 *Lady with a*

Box Bror's "unrealistic loveliness"
he & confreres inhabiting a parallel
space as in '46's *Garden of Earthly
Delights* with its teeming serpentine

3-fingered & pastel-tinctured forms
Evening Reflections of '49 with sets
of pinchers holding round or oblong
half-sliced shapes in divided shades

in '46's *The Dreamer* a nude sleeps
recumbent on the striped surface of
an altar stump outlined curvaceous
as she & on another stump a draw-

ing in blue of a man upon one knee
lifting arms as if were calling upon
some power above & yet on its top
but a pair of snails is inching along

a pelican painted on a thinner trunk
& out the lady's rotten wood mush-
rooms sprout with a head on one &
a frog on other the meaning as hard

to come by as the four-leaf clover in
Granny's yard with its vitex tempted
to the forbidden climb after a May St.
Eve whose olive skin is not forgotten

his '45 *Tree of Knowledge* reveals in-
stead of rings its two nude lovers em-
bracing as a female trio dances naked
plus four fish leaf bird & flower vase

from '45 too a *Woman Combing Her
Hair* where an oval mirror on a table
reflects her face beside an amputated
foot head hand & six fowl observing

as chickens stand about in the weeds
all as little understood as his untitled
pieces with not so living appendages
flags in '53 *Signals* can signify more

held by men in arched niches each in
variegated tights '52 *Pharmaceutical
Cabinet II* with similar architectonics
as every vial or bottle a shelf to itself

& earlier in his '45's *Cells* men push
against a wall or ceiling as undressed
woman lies with her legs spread wide
a fish pitcher crab compartmentalized

in his '60 *Fortress* chess-like pieces
only one a man head-to-foot all par-
titioned off as vessels in cubicles on
rectangular shelves in his '52 *Nun's*

Distillery as if each man woman ani-
mate thing an island after all a lonely
pigeon-holed being but if artist focus
on isolate life does comparison apply

can identify more with his '67 view
of UDLA being constructed then in
Bror's *New Buildings and Pyramid—
Cholula* for knew it later in '75-'76

with its sacred pile a cathedral sur-
mounts under a blue-pink Mexican
sky Bror reticulated after not being
drafted meant freed to etch intaglio

prints like '41 or '43 *Man in the Pit*
with a surreal dream-like "creatcher"
sits it seems on Bror's right shoulder
'44 *Strata* a soft-ground biomorphic

of an "unseen world" he manipulated
by a breathing it in more deeply even
than a shared habitat this native place
were born in though different to each

not known nor remembered the same
given facts to leave or take without or
with them to create in a simultaneous
or another time verities of each's own

in '50's *Near and Farsighted Readers*
his redhead holds her book up close to
her face while other's down in her lap
both done after able to read the letters

& words learned at George C. Clarke
elementary school where the old maid
taught this miracle too of writing them
down a debt no poetry has ever repaid

Cacti from '45 would seem the closest
he'd come to a flora or fauna of a local
kind & so changed had to refer to label
to perceive either nopal or prickly pear

Mexican Lia Cuilty's '43 untitled nude
brings Daphne to life on turning her in-
to a desertic tree & in '44 would depict
her family ranch in *The Day's at Morn*

regionalism after Thomas Hart Benton
with its fertile fields & a flock of geese
as white as their house & all their trees
filled with leaves not bare as Daphne's

yet believe it less than Cynthia Brants'
'45 *Horse and Rider* though only sat at
four on a Shetland pony for a '43 photo
in a vest & pair of chaps Granny sewed

but rather prefer her '37 *Trotting Horse*
color aquatint with lines of legs suggest
the animal's fluid motion on the printed
page & also admire later photogravures

like '83 *Shades of Times Past* origami
with weaponed men on running steeds
out of folded sheets & '82's *Trooper's
Horse* though that a bronzing of paper

unlike Bror she would both saddle up
& craft her equines to gallop & caper
with leaps & hind-leg kicks until a rid-
ing accident left her with broken back

& in a plaster cast decorated by Circle
friends who made of her a work of art
while her "elaborate bawdy jokes" re-
galed them all her spirit untamed as an

unbreakable mare a jumper responsive
to a slightest shift of equestrian weight
knee leg or hand as her show horse ex-
ecuted maneuvers intricate as her ardu-

ous process with copper plates as in her
Yesterday's Paper of '69 with its ad for
a Mobile Homes' gigantic sale wadded
up & in seventeen steps that image pre-

pared with gelatin film photo emulsion
contact exposed to the positive desired
made from a negative bathed diluted &
dissolved in acid at varied density rates

a medium well-known from portraits
Curtis took of proud aboriginal chiefs
her other '69 subjects *Low Light on a
Beach* & a moon landing *Momentous*

that shot she took from a TV screen
her '93 *A Golf Swing* recalling now
the sand traps on Colonial's course
laid out beside Trinity River banks

though never caddied on its private
fairways never played on bentgrass
after driving nine or eighteen holes
just putted eastside's public greens

yet allows for feel of a Titleist ball
she hit with her aquatint color arcs
as if by Ben Hogan's iron or wood
his follow through of body & arms

Kelly Fearing in exploring an attic
had found in '44 a shade-less lamp
a nude torso missing the porcelain
elbow-to-armpit its wires had held

he also reproducing an old newspa-
per but his on a canvas black white
& gray with headlines upside down
Germa[ny] attacks Russians Japan

invades again while two ties drape
from a hanger since missing a neck
with lives ending or interrupted by
cruel racist world gone power mad

but before the *Attic Piece* had done
in birth year his '39's *Jitterbuggers*
with its girls' swinging skirts show-
ing their knees & a red panty of one

each week back then Mom & Dad a-
waiting their drive to the city's Lake
for dancing to the big bands coming
through his favorite ever the Duke's

at times would just stand next to him
& watch as pianist with drums guitar
& bass would hit together on *Merry-
Go-Round* & also *Rockin' in Rhythm*

partial as well to Jimmie's *Lunceford
Special* with its high trumpet work &
Trummy Young on stirring trombone
Joe Thomas with that booming tenor

in those days Harry James a member
of that first band hired by the Casino
Ballroom when owner George Smith
had objected to its up-&-coming star

blasting with gusto & had its leader
seat him back behind the other men
but paid him quite a sum in years to
come for his Golden Horn out front

no need to say they would not have
driven to East Rosedale for hearing
an Ornette Coleman brand of bebop
much less his later harmolodic licks

yet neither to express any prejudice
like most from their Depression age
just didn't care for the '40s' sounds
a New Generation had begun to dig

now wonder if they had gone to see
the Circle innovations on display in
a gallery of the city's library before
it moved from Throckmorton & 9th

& if saw them there had they said a
word if they did don't retain a thing
no image at all since clearly to them
a universe as of verse were never so

curious to know not a poem nor Lia
Cuilty's *The Grapevine Swing* a fun
had later if not in '45 when she won
3rd place for her little redheaded girl

canopied by the dead austere trees
& surely not '43's *Arrested Flight*
with pink square-topped triangular-
footed cones & blue moth antennas

no such art ever appealing to them
nor clowns to entertain in Dickson
Reeder's *The Dispute* of '44 since
a pair out of its trio glares in anger

Kelly's '45 *The Kite Flyers* might
have caught an eye if knew by six
how to fly & yet the sinister white
obelisks & shapes constructed like

A's & U's must have just put off &
if unable to read the world of angry
men lying behind a comedy routine
how intuit the black in overalls pull-

ing the girlchild's happiness string
he appearing as fearful as she from
an unseen menace felt in the atmos-
phere more than in clouds or winds

while at Circle's Halloween soiree
as painted by Emily Guthrie Smith
would it have seemed funny to see
the bearded man in a casket extend-

ing his right hand to a lady in long
red dress as cowled monk with left
between his palms his face masked
administers last rites to soon-to-die

or less so tube-head figure in light-
blue cutoff nightie a fan to her lips
pointing her finger at dying painter
not at all now its minstrel Mammy

Veronica's own version of scene
in her '43 *The Host in the Coffin*
has tube head too but wears red-
&-blue tights as her hands touch

Dickson's at his & Flora's home
at 2411 6th Ave. not that far from
Granny's three-in-a-row May St.
houses Dad renting then at 3017

her two-bedroom one-bath to '49
no mansion as on Elizabeth Boul-
evard intersects with that Avenue
yet its memories rich as any there

though unrecorded in vivid colors
as the reveling of Reeders' guests
decked out in self-created get-ups
dramatized under chandelier light

one on white lace-up roller skates
holds a cane another in Hindu sari
a third at foot of winding staircase
ignores death & takes a ballet step

The Dragon and Saint George of
'37 Flora Blanc had done in Paris
a New Yorker & a Soutine model
studied with F. Léger & at Atelier

of printmaker Stanley Hayter met
her Dickson & after two had wed
came with him to his Texas home
introduced here their avant-garde

but in '46 in place of making art
she trained the children to act in
The Rose & the Ring a stage pro-
duction of Thackeray & in '48 to

do *A Midsummer Night's Dream*
with Dick designing Oberon me-
tallic costume & painting its sets
as he did for the Makepeace play

he working mostly as a portraitist
often of Circle friends as when in
'46 his best likeness proved to be
of the cerebral-palsied Bill Bomar

presses right fist against his cheek
while below his square eyeglasses
fingers of his left hand cup his ear
framing his lips mustache & beard

& captured well his fellow's eyes
peer intently through those lenses
his affliction here is under control
as when he'd pick up brush or pen

& bring to life a work in oil or ink
like his '44 painting of *Jay's Pool*
with its blue bird overlooks shim-
mering half circles & frogs swim-

ming if fish differ from Fearing's
floating in *The Aquarist* from '45
while Bill's ruffled water spreads
to the lily pad's star-white flower

as then in Granny's double pond
she cleaned in long hot summers
when barefoot cousins waded in
on those freshly sanded bottoms

for cooling off until she brought
goldfish hyacinths lilies & moss
from their washtubs back within
reddish rims of palo-pinto rocks

Bill skilled as well in portraiture
as in his *Head of an Artist* of '44
with its big dark eyes of Dickson
his receding hairline mirrored by

a black shirt collar while his '42
Santa Fe View with its chamisas
& Apache plumes can   fill a need
for that landscape of near & dear

but if he did include such plants
by his water-color crosshatches &
dots it will take a closer look for
verifying that familiar sight

seen with María on visits there
had meant so very much to her
since New Mexico adobe walls
could return the ones she knew

in her idyllic Chilean childhood &
acequias too reminded of one ran
through her Granddad's par-cel of
land when in rubber boots

he irrigated grapevines & avoca-
do & his vegetable garden same
as Uncle Alvin's & yet here un-
welcomed by her mother-in-law

had wanted a different daughter
when she as good as gold to her
who was never deserving of her
who gave up her own birthplace

to come to this for the native son
whose Cowtown with its abattoir
odious to her yet then would find
Aunt Sis like her in mind & heart

both delighted in antique treasure
others considered junk & enjoyed
to learn from her of family names
of Great Uncle Earl photographed

in his derby hat with roguish leer
shown in the 3019 May St. home
where Sis & Al raised their three
& partly a nephew just next door

then spending one weekend here
she'd discover at the museums of
Kimbell & Carter the recompense
of their exhibitions of timeless art

Dallas

encircled by freeway loops
has wished itself a Roman arena
but styled more after Texas Stadium
where gladiators   this time
Christians from Abilene or SMU
take on Lions Bears & Rams
while the lawyer-merchant class
spies down day & night
from box seats through tinted glass
spots the animals in goal-line stands
or in last ditches along skid row
below
too are those looking for his-
tory   staring at tobacco stains on
Federal Building walks   visitors in from Boston
wondering
Is this where our hero bled?
buying his souvenirs   windows Xed
in snapshots where Oswald took his aim
his bullets granting one more wish

such carpet rides lift powerlines
overpasses skyscrapers high
rises hopes of masses   recall
how they were raised for
days   driving here as a family when fall
trips to the State Fair were long & hard
where at last in Sears would try
on the cowboy boots had wanted so   like Gene's
or Roy's   but with narrow feet
Dad said no   they didn't fit

nothing in Dallas ever does
it's Texas but then it's not
it isn't the West   it never was
would have it moved to an eastern spot

partly this comes out as
the talk of a Cowtown boy   Fort Worth-Dallas
called twin cities yet rivals from the start

the real Texas   with cattle & horses
rodeos at Will Rogers Coliseum   versus
the Airport

typical of towns grown near   the closest father & son
born to carry a rivalry on
Darío's red head sticks
out in any crowd
can be a pain   yet will claim him any time
like all of Texas   or so would rhyme

Big D's a sore thumb too
though giving credit where credit's due
both share winning points
this city can boast of parks & lakes
are a blue-green sketch
for him to sit & draw   match
with watercolor or tempera paints
outdo this description   make a Papa proud

carry him back to creeks shaded
by pecan & peach   running clear & cold
over smooth & green-furred rocks   fresh
by willows   in summer a cool conversing   traded
for memos typed at the Apparel Mart   to baskets sold
beside the bridge   their priceless wrinkled pits
brown-black nuts fallen at feet once bared to rip-
ples   rainbow perch   a movement Darío can better catch

need for that his art   need his love
needed Love Field too   a where to land
& seek for him athletic fun   a high-
er flight than had on fleetest jets   a swim-
ming hole for deeper dives than
dips on tollway drives   a where to buy
western boots for the skinny kid
right for walking streets can still recov-
er a magic word will trim shed blood
like a genii whisked
back inside an olym-
pic lamp over-rubbed

Castroville

taking Interstate 35
Onderdonk's bluebonnets still in bloom
we skirted the Alamo City on loop 410
an easy air-conditioned drive

      to where in 1866 Mother St. Andrew arrived
      three shipwrecks in all she alone survived
      the first Sisters having set sail in '63
      long before access road or superhighway

      Father Dubuis who burned with zeal
      brought them over on the St. Geneviève
      up the coast through hunger & exposure
      by bogs & swollen rivers past Civil War

      holding in heavy rains their violins
      bringing their song to these barren plains
      against dread scarlet or typhoid fever
      monstrance chalice & statues of saints

      La Coste then the closest rail connection
      five miles away & at flood time marooned
      where today its tacky restored train station
      now features a sauna & a swimming pool

then heading west on highway 90
having come from Austin without a single stop
we hit the light here at Landmark Inn
the Parks & Wildlife running it then

      racked by Lipan & Comanche raids
      with poisoned arrows ending in hooks
      were not to be pulled from any victim
      even more her Bishop's ambitious barbs

      treated worse than any convict or slave
      evicted from a house her own sweat raised
      with nowhere to go none to give her refuge
      & neither was her life her own to take

        blamed for her brother Father Feltin's arrest
        each night of exile for those twenty years
        wetting her pillow with tears of remorse
        even undergoing surgery with nothing for pain

        in part to repay others for sorrows she brought
        a blessed sacrifice made in her guiltless state
        then at last in the Sisters' cemetery laid to rest
        at the foot of the mountain still known as Cross

came the time before in December
now returning in April to number 8
this room a favorite with newlyweds
in 1940 being termed a smokehouse

a one-story before shots were fired at Sumter
the upper floor added as a bathhouse
tradition says the only spot to bathe
between San Antonio & Eagle Pass

out this open door
once a window
the pecans' new green
framed as if a picture

        like one of Rowena Vance's primitive scenes
        Vermont schoolmarm painted this Inn
        her husband John's hotel circa 1857
        put his name on it above the entrance

        with to the left a picket fence
        in the foreground some chickens
        from the back a girl in a pinafore
        alongside what is perhaps a dog

        bushy trees swayed by
        an invisible breeze
        a tie-rail perhaps
        for the traveler's horse

through the wire mesh see branches' shadows
dappling the sunlight on the distant roof
of the Haass-Quintle gristmill
rippled with rust

between here & its limestone walls
white rails of the painted porch
with between those & here
black squares of the patterned screen

    her correspondence & records destroyed
    by Bishop Neraz knifed the pages
    crumpled & lit them in a wire burner
    the fire a reflection of his beaming face

    as flames licked their edges
    blackened the leaves to ash
    her score of years consumed
    two decades of success heartache failure

    upholding the rule of enclosure
    keeping cattle out of the grapes
    her dowry spent for teaching French
    for burning of learning's midnight oil

    deposed for saying just what she meant
    for accusing clergy of seeking diversion
    for not trusting recreation with lonely priests
    had driven their foundress away in disgrace

    mostly an excuse to separate the Order
    from its congregation back in Alsace
    to make Divine Providence a Texas branch
    diocesan with the final word up to Neraz

    she the first to travel afar
    followed in Father Moye's steps
    he in China doing missionary work
    seized & dragged into a mandarin's court

    there his vestments torn & trampled
    decreed would be set afire but all along he believed
    they had secretly kept them knowing their worth
    in denying he hid a Bible lied as St. Peter had

a whole history focused upon
this screen door in early spring
viewed from this old four poster
beneath its ceiling a cistern before

pentagonal at first & lined with lead
then Rebs peeled & melted it down
molding bullets for invading Yanks
to rout them or leave them dead

filled from the river by hydraulic pump
big enough for three to bathe at once
heated by a fireplace on the floor below
now lie here so grateful she never did

who planned to after attending retreats
following Padre Pedro her mentor then
precious needlework her nanny had learned
from this Order in Temuco had taken her in

who took María to mass in Mary's month
bought for her the sprigs of baby's breath
to carry to the altar with its sweet incense
afterwards no service would she ever miss

like Sister Arsene who accompanied Mother
who had to leave her rosary & her ring behind
María giving up the veil & her beloved Chile
for poverty & primeval solitude of a Texas kind

can see her observing the postulant's rules
silence in dormitories   no talk at the table
darkened halls & dusky basements & maybe
homesick & despondent as Sister Clemence

> who could not adjust to the language & life
> set out on foot for Danville eight miles distant
> in the woods between New Braunfels & Solms
> her habit found intact but only on bones

> not alone the triple scourge those Sisters endured
> of Indian deprivation   cholera   & drought
> Mother St. Andrew deprived even of holy communion
> for being the Bishop said disobedient

María untrammeled & of her own free will
never to kneel at his pontifical throne
though wonder now does she ever regret
not having chosen chastity's perpetual robes

envious as the devil to envision her there
her lovely head bared & bowed to his fingers
purified for lifting a strand of her hair
for the investiture had forbidden forever

then led to the room & clothed for him
as the choir chanted by candlelight *Te Deum*
after the ceremony as sign of new dignity assumed
to receive flower wreath & his caress of peace

jealous even knowing of the crying need
for such virgin brides to comfort & teach
to practice their frugal unworldly ways
wishing always & ever to have her alone

for this view to where they built their mill
giving to their village its industrial mien
so Alsatian the tourist cannot conceive
he's in Texas on Henri's farming grant

his camp made underneath that dormant pecan
near Apache hunting grounds & dinosaur tracks
where smooth metal pulleys & cast-iron gear shafts
sent water by tunnel to grind their cotton & corn

Jewish-Portuguese-Frenchman allowed who owed
to repay him by working on their church & school
while longing for the Rhine & their city of bells
where their azure pottery adorned its market stalls

begrudge them her even knowing their then & now
on having to share the bed with how many nuptials
as the Medina swirls in among those cypress knees
reach to hers to locks unravished by religious vows

Burnet

Dad had driven here to have an excuse
for those born & raised there is no choice
though given one later many will choose

never to leave even such a godforsaken place
since wherever it is is where the memories are made
will stay on for any through whatever loss

each season the scoring run or pass replayed
from a game won district or a regional cup
in the report filed by Detective Wade

the fellow known as Ben had suddenly turned up
to tell a tale of both his parents dead
the local vet who gave him a job one more dupe

to that double murder the orphan said
happened near Detroit when he was just 13
later a high school dropout who had hit the road

this town of thirty-five hundred taken in
by that vagabond arrested Monday on a burglary charge
all those who had given him a standing ovation

at the ceremony for scholarship awards
as a senior a full one from A & M
but after graduation a suspected robber of barns

the vet still recalls the day he came
a clean-looking kid in need of a break
did well on any & every exam

his B.S. in animal science nothing fake
but with thieving & his mother alive in Poplar Bluff
he & the others rued their farewell BBQ   putting faith

in any such tragic past   one more than enough
to warm Hill Country hearts now hard & cool
to the thought of ever again being so generous

their applauding hands now feeling the fool
as for Dad he had only driven here to buy a necktie
his reason maybe as much against the Golden Rule

as the Michigan homicides in that drifter's lie
yet his ruse had made that vacation come true
& so in a boyhood mind far easier to justify

the family stay in '48 at nearby Lake Bu-
chanan can always outweigh in any balance
his visit-to-a-dry-goods-store subterfuge

the alibi of a seller of life insurance
invented so his boss would think he was here on business
while spending a week with wife kids cousins uncles & aunts

sleeping in a camper he had bought for so much less
than he said it was worth though vented wrong
for any air to reach to that thin sweaty mattress

on those sultry nights so hot & endlessly long
the hours an eternity on awaiting signs of morning light
even dared to brave mosquitoes outside & watch for dawn

through every real or imagined sound or shadowy sight
beyond the yellow glow cast by that driftwood fire
drew nearer to its needless heat in wondrous fright

preferring such fear to that closer safer trailer
Dad's scheme later to load it with Christmas toys
hauled & peddled house to house in a Radio Flyer

while he would sell town-to-town his terms & twenty-pays
hitting the telephone operators & department stores
Mom always reminding him how only his boys

sold enough with innocent faces at neighbors' doors
to let him break even & empty that camper in time to move
to Altus where it disappeared though not from these shores

have come to now for the Vanishing Texas Cruise
forty years later a return trip to this river where
in its man-made lake the same sunken trees still lose

their branches as they bob up as if for air
rising to float at the rippled surface
as thoughts of a father & an aunt both gone forever

now ease up here in their boat & cast for crappie or bass
to set or check their trotlines by the lantern's light
as fluttering wings ping the Coleman's sooty glass

dying to enter its flame-filled bag still burning bright
on Rosalyn who suffered so many years before her end
who fished with Guy from Alaska to Amazon day or night

knew the deep seas from Azores to Thailand
wherever the Air Force stationed their handsome
son   Dad testing irrigation canal or a farmer's tank

with his stinking balls of bait he would concoct at home
caught nothing more exotic than gar or gasper-goo
lost minnows or worms to a mess of throwaway bream

hooked mostly mud or channel cats yellow or blue
but patient with pole & equally with rod & reel
or while he made his calls let wind carry a rubber balloon

out to the middle of that city lake these scenes reveal
here where Fall Creek has emptied for half-a-million years
In just one their count has doubled Mike begins his tour-guide spiel

on steaming by cliffs with claret cup cactus & prickly pear
on this beautiful 75-degree February day
with the sky above the Colorado sunny & clear

on its 600-mile journey to Matagorda Bay
In the deepest spot the lake is 45 feet the river 12 to 15
This boat drafts two & a half & comes equipped with a galley

Captain Al & I hope we can spot a few of the 17
to 35 American eagles   but he fears the fishing fest
with its outboard motors may frighten them off   If golden

they're immature if black with white heads
full grown They differ in their flat-wing
flight from the v-shaped wobble of buzzards build their nests

right on the ground & leave when eagles show up to eat rodents
& fish Never kill no cattle though ranchers shoot the bald
Confuse it with the golden Them there's double-crested cormorants

astompin' their feet & aflappin' their wings On your left's Seldom Falls
one o' their favorite haunts The cedar here about's so thick
it chokes the ranch grass but resists any fire Live oak roots go down tall

as the tree itself Reach to the river through limestone strips
That great blue heron's astandin' in driftwood beer cans & trash
& that there's ball moss It won't kill the tree Lives on air like orchids

Up ahead before we turn around at Deer Creek we'll be a-pass-
in' Buzzard Roost   but dock without spotting wingspans 6 to 7 feet
then drive back by outcrops of green glauconite & on to Burnet's

namesake where Elisa ran her four- & eight-hundred meters
at the gun sprinting for the tape   Burnet it was fired the very first shot
to free the whole South American continent   on her final kick beat

the field   won two medals even with shin splints   he at times boxed
in as when on her birthday May 20th underneath the brightest of stars
he signed Velasco Treaty & spared Santa Anna when others were hot

on stringing him up   after Miranda betrayed the revolution   Bolívar's
that is   David struck by pulmonary consumption & crossed the Sabine
in search of health   lived ten years with Comanches restored his vigor

avoiding ardent spirits subsisting on hunted game
said racing their favorite amusement their democracy
most perfect on earth little harmony in their deliberating

then engrafted the vices of civilized life all too readily
those who rescued the president-elect from a premature grave
he later presiding over the first court session before the machinery

flat played out   his eldest lost in Civil War   poor & desolate yet saved
those horsemen's sounds for heavens plants & man:
Muur paam-pee phee paa-ve Taa-ve

ha-nebe sau-nipp so-co-vete ta-bane tucan
a "species" cut off who took him in while they to "melt away
an untimely vernal snow   inscrutable in their origin"

fluent in Spanish "unique in habits wild & uncultivated
but in no wise deficient in intellectual endowments"
"encroached" on at last by a "disastrous" race *"unsocial & depraved"*

both these & those proved gracious hosts   the difference
more in their guests   one a wobbly errant bird
the other by generosity of spirit soared to eminence

as for Dad if deceptive still in buying that tie he kept his word

Baird

after Early Days in Callahan County (ca. 1966)
by Brutus Clay Chrisman

Prologue

are there no more stories to tell
none has come to mind
& why is that

they used to show up on their own
or would easily call them up
but now it seems

they're done with me or I myself
have run out of things to say
& yet the world goes right on

something new every day
& the old themes are still around
& are just as good as they ever were

loyalty & betrayal
the arts like music
jazz & classical

all should still inspire
but somehow they
have lost their power

to move to words
as they did before
in stanzas long or short

in free form or rhyming patterns
couplets quatrains tercets cinquains
& behold the next-to-last

have come again
despite a feeling
they never would

the fault not theirs
but mine alone for know
of all I've written

how little or nothing
can still hold up
while the others' poems

will always read
with renewed delight
Chaucer's *Troilus & Criseyde*

a Boccaccio tale from Trojan days
retold in Geoffrey's royal rime
but why repeat it

or any other
since many a plot
lies ready at hand

like the one for years
has gone on haunting
yet avoided from fear

could not believably enter
or should not
its dark disturbing past

its history of one
took another's life
till now at last

have gone ahead
& as a college prof had said
am doing it for myself

to learn a lesson or two
or none
getting it down

even if no one
picks it up
or if any should

but drops it after
a single line
will revisit that tragic time

not to condemn or pardon
but to listen to & live with
if never to understand

Relations

soon after the century turned
Grandad moved his family here
to this railroad shipping point
with roundhouse shops & yard
among mesquite & prickly pear

he coupling & uncoupling cars
lifting levers for switching tracks
signaling with lantern or flag
through heat wave & norther
as wildflowers bloomed in spring

ten years after they came
the 1905 train station replaced
by the 1911 Prairie-style brick
with overhanging eaves' decorative belt
Flemish-like parapet & low-pitched roof

its wide horizontal architectural look
a reaction against the vertical
assembly-line mass-produced Greek & Roman
intended to appear as if
grown naturally from scrubby plain

known for its antique stores
a dozen lining Market Street
& for 1912's runaway engine
caused three locomotives to collide
more than for 1907's hanging

Callahan County's one & only
among legally last in State
eight years later daddy born
delivered by Dr. Robert Griggs
cured with his own concoction

the flu cases of '17
gave it over the phone
to patients free of charge
though nothing dad had mentioned
since then a two-year old

nor spoke of that execution
just remembered riding his mule
to a Boy Scouts meeting
with his dime to join
but was not let in

if aware of that event
it could not have been
from newspaper headlines of 1906
on young Emma Blakely murdered
nor of 1907's justice done

maybe later his folks recounted
their sitting in county's courtroom
listening to witnesses or testifying
agreeing with verdict & sentence
or perhaps having different views

only came myself in 2001
in search of relatives recorded
in the courthouse's basement library
perhaps in some centennial volume
but located not a trace

just that history unknown before
with names of those concerned
on display in yellowed clippings
in a dusty see-through case
the crime with reasons why

Alberto Vargas

nothing have read has said
what had brought him here
in one letter he wrote
fate had played a role

whether he hopped a boxcar
or alighted from a coach
or made it on foot
no one seemed to know

after he arrived in 1906
in late or early spring
no address is given for
where he was living then

since that letter also states
it would shock the boarders
perhaps he roomed in housing
Texas & Pacific had built

to attract the immigrants west
yet Mexican migrants traveled north
& crossed against the law
helped construct the railroad lines

drove spikes in creosote-coated ties
while Europeans would enter through
New York & Galveston ports
mostly welcomed with open arms

if he not warmly received
found work at Sigal Hotel
washing dishes in its restaurant
would turn eighteen in May

described as quiet & pleasant
could communicate in basic English
though not enough to express
his passion for his waitress

A Rancher

his death didn't satisfy us
since witnesses standing in front
kept us from seeing him
up on the platform planks
of the tall stockade-like gallows

in a clear solemn voice
Sheriff Irvin read the sentence
Judge Calhoun had pronounced before
when the jury found him
guilty in the first degree

at that time in November
a month after killing her
he had heard his punishment
& said it was right
that he wanted to die

on January 4th in handcuffs
after stepping forward to speak
his last words on earth
he waited until the crowd
pressed forward & quieted down

then unhesitating he calmly declared
he would unite with her
& after that everything happened
far too fast as Sheriff
pulled tight on the rope

the trap door opened &
the boy's own body weight
dropped him down to where
few could watch the deputies
by turns taking his pulse

on feeling none they informed
the Committee & sent word
to the Sheriff who took
a deep breath everyone heard
then let go the rope

but later cut the noose
not to leave a souvenir
& placed its knotted loop
inside the box with him
& hammered down the lid

with coffin on a wagon
the deputies seated on top
the Sheriff drove the horses
to Ross Cemetery's unmarked grave
as the townspeople drifted away

we ranchers were all disgusted
that instead of being able
to string him up ourselves
the Sheriff had learned beforehand
we were riding into Baird

coming in from Eagle Cove
where that girl's family lived
but before we even arrived
Sheriff took him to Abilene
& after returning to town

announced without batting an eye
Vargas was going to receive
a fair & impartial trial
then headed home to sleep
while we ranted & raved

A Citizen

with the Clyde telephone wires
buzzing the news
a few of us
commandeered a T&P freight

took it east to the county seat
but in the night
a posse & buggy
bypassed us going back to the west

only at the station did we find
Sheriff Irvin & his men
had whisked away that spic
keeping him safe in Abilene

how could those lawmen
protect such scum
we should close the border
keep them from coming in

they only steal rape & murder
while we pay taxes
so their kids can attend
our expensive schools for free

they reproduce like rabbits
& speak no English
sure they work the fields
for not much pay

but they take good jobs away
from those are legally here
I say send them back
& put up a wall

Sheriff Al Irvin

Doc Grizzard feared
with Alberto's wounds
he wouldn't survive
the 25 miles
from Baird to
Abilene's county jail

but I knew
if the mob
ever got aholt
of him he
would swing from
the nearest tree

if he lived
to have his
day in court
it would do
right by him
& would also

protect the town
from a lawless
reputation by giving
proof that here
too justice is
served & besides

the railroad surely
would have disapproved
would have shut
this junction down
as the company
threatened to do

when it sent
that Negro family
whose father operated
the coal chute
& no one
ever bothered them

& they lived
among us with
not one incident
so I say
think first of
the community's good

The Jailor's Wife

once they brought him back to Baird
to await his trial
I chatted with him
on taking meals up to his cell

I saw a woman's presence comforted him
& began to feel
what a gentle spirit
was there inside his skin & bones

couldn't conceive he'd done such a thing
it seemed he never
would've harmed a fly
much less in cold blood murdered her

he never complained just spoke of her
& one time asked
for pencil & paper
& drew a beautiful picture of her

I let the custodian's children visit him
& he fashioned toys
from materials they brought
& he became a friend to them

their father told them when he died
& it saddened them
to lose their friend
who patiently listened to their endless prattle

I told my husband of his sweetness
but he warned me
not to be naïve
to trust no man behind the bars

in his experience he had often seen
a woman would credit
anything a prisoner said
would even fall in love with him

one tried to help a prisoner escape
felt sorry for him
said Don't be deceived
if he gets away he'll kill again

during his last hours his lawyer came
& with him too
was the Clyde priest
who spoke with & prayed with him

& then the Sheriff entered his cell
& around his wrists
snapped shiny new cuffs
below those of his jacket's faded sleeves

in denim pants & a blue shirt
a nice dressy necktie
the priest beside him
he was ready to meet his Maker

but just before he left the cell
he asked that I
for being so kind
be given his pencil drawing of her

Dallas Scarborough

since I had worked in Baird before
for my attorney uncle B.L. Russell
just after I was admitted to the bar
the Judge appointed me as counsel

of my 200 murder cases were tried
I'd lose no other in my long career
at least by execution no client died
none sentenced more than 20 years

once I argued before the Appellate
& the Justices who heard that case
all favored moving the county seat
I lost that appeal & the courthouse

while a student of the law in Austin
I'd played baseball at the University
got a pro contract but turned it down
thought it beneath a lawyer's dignity

in football starred at defensive tackle
yet 03-04 we won no championships
embarrassed by an all-Indian Haskell
but that loss not near so painful as his

as first coach at now Hardin-Simmons
I don't recall losing but a single game
a Big D parochial school won that one
yet prefer it over such a grievous fame

from the first I knew we wouldn't win
for talking with him it was clear to me
I couldn't be successful defending him
not even on the grounds of his insanity

for he was thoughtful as a person can be
he told me he could not live without her
& on learning she was another's fiancée
had knifed her & himself to die together

if I had had even a little more experience
I was after all just six years older than he
I might have worked up a strong defense
but none would have convinced that jury

even though two men in Clyde had filed
for a change of venue based on prejudice
it was soon denied when the Sheriff held
there was not at all any evidence of such

but when I asked each prospective juror
whether he'd scruple if he had to inflict
a death penalty every flint-eyed rancher
looked at him & replied "NOT A BIT!"

later it would become my firm convic-
tion that jurors can be depended upon
to deliver an honest fair & just verdict
& jury trial's a democratic cornerstone

I also came to conclude that every man
who has served on a jury & woman too
will afterwards become a better citizen
& even in his case it was probably true

on that crisp fall morning 20 November
courtroom & courthouse's halls as well
overflowed with the spectators so eager
to view in action Law's avenging angel

after Judge Calhoun had called for order
& prosecution made its opening remarks
I pled his age even knowing long before
it wouldn't change those minds or hearts

of 35 witnesses the State put on the stand
most swore they were in the dining room
& as she entered he had followed behind
turned her about to stab her in the bosom

some recalled a terrified look on her face
when she saw him holding a paring knife
& all had heard a sudden frightened gasp
as she tried to break away & save her life

but she staggered & slumped to the floor
as each diner sat on entranced & hushed
while he jabbed at his chest over & over
until he fell on her when they all rushed

to her side & on not feeling a heartbeat
one doctor there gently closed her eyes
then the bleeding boy audibly breathed
& found alive was seized with outcries

dragged to the jail down Market Street
& as those witnesses had told & retold
their gruesome details no one believed
that jury to vote for life without parole

& so I'd decide not to have him testify
being certain then it would do no good
& in spite of the State's long testimony
by afternoon Judge Calhoun instructed

the jury to retire & consider the verdict
was never in doubt for not one moment
& in almost no time they returned with
guilty & their now-banned punishment

the Judge then called for Alberto to rise
& said if he wanted he now could speak
when all ears would listen with surprise
to his sincere voice though he still weak

from wounds by then had not yet healed
as he thanked the jury in broken English
for their decision was not to be appealed
since death not prison had been his wish

with the date set for execution it seemed
a load lifted from his shoulders as calm-
ly he stood up straight looking redeemed
& shook my hand yet that to me no balm

for I have never lived down my only loss
since in all the cases I would later defend
clients served little time or had gotten off
& all the defendants I took were innocent

Zacatecas

for Baird had traded his birthplace
with its mines still active then
the Eden & Our Lady's Remedies
among richest in all New Spain
worked first when Chichimecans came
to dominate its hilly semi-desert terrain

their gold & silver deposits erected
the baroque cathedral of pink sandstone
with Solomonic columns portals & naves
its sculpted Christ & Virgin Mary
in its flank niches Four Evangelists
cherubs caryatids vines & acanthus leaves

its plaza & winding cobbled streets
with one alleyway called Sadhearted Indian
after the 1548 tale of Xolótl
who loved the last Chichimecan princess
though Xúchitl rejected him & wed
Gonzalo de Tolosa the Spanish captain

in the temple ruins of Tlacuitlapán
the desperate Xolótl watched from above
their procession to the Chapel Mexicapán
losing all faith in the gods
dying emaciated still holding a flower
the meaning of her Nahuatl name

crusading missionaries trekked north from here
with its monasteries schools & seminary
markets offering leather crafts & silverworks
guavas grapes & *aguamiel* of agave
the cafés with trumpeting mariachi bands
opera house theater & teachers' college

he departing for this little-known spot
passed through by rails & cattle
mostly only shoppers for antiques stop
unlike his city where tourists arrive
to view the tribes & architecture
survive in its now UNESCO site

why then had he ever left
not from Revolution would only come
when Villa captured its fortified hills
El Grillo & then La Bufa
Pancho's greatest victory over Federal troops
seven years after Alberto was hung

his complexion once described as dark
perhaps he was partly an aborigine
not then ethnic nor drug-war refugee
reportedly he attended quality schools
his written Spanish correct & expressive
evident from letters addressed to her

no photo either confirms or denies
if he was handsome or unattractive
if comely girls of Hispanic blood
Zacatecan or a mixture of two
would have turned from his embrace
or did he seek another race

of lighter skin & thinner limbs
of the blonde & blue-eyed kind
or instead of leaving for them
had it been for another place
for a job with decent pay
one with a future more secure

did he even intend to stay
or was he waiting to save
enough to continue north or east
to Fort Worth or farther on
in search of his American dream
or had he come from wanderlust

& then while soaping the plates
he saw her with her tray
serving the customers food & drink
& after that no other plan
nothing else would do for him
but having her for his own

Emma Blakely

in sensational news of my death
nearly nothing was written of me
other than being active in church
attending Sunday school & Sunday service
& waiting on tables at Sigal's
nothing of my family or fiancé

to have them left in peace
& me buried in Eagle Cove
is all I would have wished
but in his pocket they found
letters he never passed to me
in his language I couldn't read

those letters keep my memory alive
yet how can I ever accept
for having taken my life away
to live by his amorous words
tell of my figure attracted him
how I wounded his unworthy soul

gossip hinted the attention he paid
must have been amusing to me
but meeting him in the kitchen
I only smiled to be polite
too busy keeping up with orders
to take any notice of him

& besides I was happily engaged
to my Texas & Pacific brakeman
& we would soon be married
till suddenly he whirled me around
to face that blade he held
& plunged repeatedly into my breast

each time I shouted within myself
why do you hate me so
how ever imagine he worshipped me
& would try to slay himself
to be interred along with me
his cruel way of revering me

how believe in such a thing
no text I had ever known
no sermon I had ever heard
blessed a union based in sin
it would only belong in hell
never on earth or heaven above

how had I ever wronged him
never once did I encourage him
nor was ever unkind to him
how did I deserve to die
at the hands of a madman
I barely knew before that day

oh Scriptures teach us to forgive
those who have trespassed against us
how hard to learn that lesson
to put His command in practice
for each to love one another
as he did in murdering me

The Letters

my dearest love before your innocence
I'm a mean & rotten thing
I'm even worse than a dog
if you only knew the wounds
you open in my lonely soul
when you smile on another man

I am unworthy even to kiss
the earth your feet have touched
I'm beneath your blood & class
oh those are life's great differences
& rarely can we ever see
why our feelings come to us

what pain it gives to me
to tell you the horrible thought
has entered my head this night
the shock that it will cause
to your family & boarders here
oh such an awful bloody thought

I can already see your face
& can hardly bear its terror
it hurts & yet it fascinates
I know in this terrible affair
you will not believe my love
can mix good fortune with misery

you will think such a deed
can only have come from bitterness
not from the greatness of love
& yet the latter is true
for I have felt my dear
only the deepest devotion to you

o my darling oh Emma mine
you are & will forever be
the dearest love life's given me
I wish you would understand me
& I could show to you
how little it means to me

to leave this always unfair world
since I'll die within your arms

your lips up close to mine
remembering how you smiled at me
how slender your arms & legs
yet unluckily not knowing the pain

your being would bring to me
though resentment I have never felt
nor ever saw it in you
o do know my virgin angel
for only a moment in life
I loved & adored you so

but finding you would marry another
envy would have reduced me to
a homeless bum on the street
o who's to blame for this
my having to take your life
o destiny's it is destiny's fault

whenever you would gaze at others
I knew you would never return
the looks I gave to you
who knows what will happen now
may our bodies remain as one
hearts & souls in warming sun

* * *

Baird October 19 1906

Mrs. Praxedïs Saldivar
Zacatecas

Dearest Mother receive this final letter
& grant your son your blessing
you will never imagine my sorrow
in having to tell you now
by the time these words arrive
I may lie under the earth

Do commend my soul to God
& impart to the family members
this news I send from Baird
& with nothing further to say
I here sign myself as ever
your beloved loving son A Vargas

Epilogue

once born in
or moved to
this Texas town

one may choose
to remain or
leave as Grandma

did when she
took the kids
to Cowtown for

that city's benefits
Grandad staying for
his railway job

living it is
said in a
shack until he

passed while others
may stay for
the place itself

its easy routine
its familiar scene
its bluebonnet springs

had Alberto left
on having learned
Emma loved another

& returned to
Zacatecas to waste
away holding in

his hand not
a knife but
as had Xolótl

a harmless flower
& let her
with her brakeman

live their life
together would his
future not have

held one as
precious as she
or might he

by drawing &
writing of all
her charms not

have come to
discover those in
art or poem

had Dad not
gone with Grandma
& married someone

other than Mom
would I never
have been &

not have seen
clippings & Chrisman
would lead to

these indebted lines
have tried to
revive their shortened

lives such questions
remain unanswered as
Alberto surely knew

who himself had
written of how
"anyone is liable

to do it
at any time
and any moment

if they too
get into the
same fix that

I was in"
but even having
the answer right

one may fail
to follow through
if not to

commit a crime
of passion yet
to make the

loved one suffer
instead of sacrificing
one's selfish love

from *Austin: a Poem*

Sabine

that first semester here & as it should began
on this street furthest east in Waller's plan
where Andy had picked out the fanciest pad
shared with Gordon who ducked out early
for the old Music Building's recital hall
to practice on the organ reserved for then
or so he'd claim when his turn had come
to do the dishes   huge feet (*patudo* in Chile)
a mystery how he played one pedal at a time

but was needed to meet that higher rent
though Andy offered to pay the difference
for that apartment too expensive for two
could not believe their invasion at night
when a sudden flash lit its one long room
as he screamed & leapt straight up in bed
so certain was struck by a lightning bolt
but said he'd awakened & suddenly felt
a giant rat sitting right on his chest

unaffected by mouse traps set out for them
they would saunter off after eating the cheese
with a broom beat them off the garbage sacks
called the landlord said Just pinch their necks
then later brought over his steel-toothed claws
to catch them coming out through every hole
in that luxury apartment's limestone walls
would not have had them with cheaper rates
yet remembered more from the promise made

after seeing an e.e. imitation in a display case
Bass's "o orange water lily" had won 1st place
in reaction the urge born to respond one day
how another's prize was to open the way
from that hall in Parlin to her Chilean face
in '79 to follow in his footsteps at the HRC
working as Jim Bagg's editorial assistant
being saved from selling shoes with a Ph.D.
starts given by Bob's win & the job he quit

his poem from *Corral* in that hallway exhibit
across from one with Eckman's double sonnet
both outside the office door of Mody Boatright
Chairman of English when he would shuffle in
to that class was taking on the Age of Darwin
ash from his stogie flaking before it fell away
or chewed too short & soggy to light it again
his lecture on Hawthorne's prairie conflagration
indelible as a fire-resistant Bible's asbestos say

another on social evolution of Wm. Graham Sumner
declared the struggle for survival a condition of man
poverty not to be abolished by the passing of laws
but by working each day that the weak grow strong
typed a term paper on Progress at that kitchen bar
while overhead the Neanderthals stomped & rolled
a cave entrance rock or some outsized mixing bowl
another mystery now segues from this river street
to its namesake when a freshman attending Lamar

crossed it then with Burkart's Brass Ensemble
for a performance at LSU in Baton Rouge
of that joyous piece Paul Holmes composed
in Beaumont in '58   he Abilene born in '23
studied theory here in the old music rooms
just a stone's throw away from Guadalupe
his pock-marked face   hands so large
a man of gangly build & a sallow skin
his notes so vibrant so warm & clear

such care he took to copy them out
each player's part in manuscript
with stems & rests a match in ink
for his sound so infectious so elegant
conveyed by every ringing phrase
his penmanship that even made
the tricky upbeat rhythms
his sudden acrobatic leaps
all somehow to come out right

the shock of discord never his way
reason enough his work is rarely heard
would admit to liking Hindemith a bit
mostly fugues & sarabands of J.S. Bach

never listened much to his fellow composers
feared drowning he said in the influence pool
Andy considered it a sinking not to swim
both then standing as guardian angels
each whispering a differing what to do
had heard the others & hear them still
their hows & whys of all these lines
any hope this poem may stay afloat
so dependent on each & everyone
as much on Estevan's life & letters
for launching again where & when
those student friends had rented then
once more their lives & voices lifting
this writing seeks to keep them current

Holmes who wrote for harmony more
than for any thought of fame or glory
& the same holds true for Estevan too
as when in '26 with things still touch & go
he sent his warning to both bickering sides
to swallow pride & lay their arms aside
addressing his hard but friendly epistles
to a self-styled commandant had just as he
after tedious waiting won a grant to settle

pero nada que ver con él
this Edwards whose impudence brought
an outpouring of the public's protest
from those had long before he came
found that spot held a greater promise
had forded their wives & kids & hogs
across this stream   their same Sabine
has named this redivivus river street
later the Louisiana-Texas dividing line

near Nacogdoches along this side
with its banks forever shaded by
dogwood sweetgum   red & white pine
announced he would send them back again
have every squatter bound in chains
his threats he bragged a hurricane
the Spaniards he branded an idle lot
stirred the Indians to join his band
for running those "foreigners" off

bribed their chieftains Mush & Bowl
declared their sacred burial grounds
a Republic where free men could reign
the Mexican government he shouted down
till then he & his followers forced to flee
sent packing by their own red flags
their rhetoric of a thundering storm
hightailing it across the same Sabine
their typhoon talk tamed by Estevan's oil

his words to any listening ear
no truer music will one ever hear
a concord recalled by this river street
its name recording that time & place
when tempers ran a raging tempest
floodwaters of cacophonous cries
a drowning out of all common sense
till calmed by the warm clear tones
of Estevan's admonishing prose

in turn reminds of that composer's notes
his "Lento for Tuba and Piano"
a piece inspired by Robert LeBlanc
student switched from a lucrative career
as chemical or a petroleum engineer
to that instrument awkward & slow
though with diaphragm under control
could hold his breath then boom it out
to pump to life Holmes' song & dance

as Estevan too had held it in
his counsel kept but then released
in measured phrases render still
his advice so sound & soothing

"I would write directly
to the Governor of the State
Give him a full statement of facts
and a very minute history of the acts

Write in *English* and make an apology
for doing so   It is perhaps
a fortunate thing I have learned patience
in the hard School of an Empresario

for I assure you
that in this place
I have had full use
of all I possessed

Gaines and a few others
blamed Ahumada and me
for the course I advised
Fields and Hunter

are certainly killed
by the Cherokees
and all the other leaders
of his fanatic party

have escaped across the Sabine
and I advised a mild course
with those who were compromitted
in a secondary degree

Ahumada chose to pursue it
and for this a few blame me
but I have a consolation
worth more than the approbation

of any and the Mexican character stands higher now
than it ever did before   I hope the people of the Colony
will be satisfied   for *theirs* is worth more to me
than all the world besides"

remembered it all through Holmes
whose very music evokes Estevan
forgotten there in his distant cell

in '22 had first come over
in dark as to his *Lively's* fate
having left before he even knew

the company & its cargo landed safe
feared those aboard that ship
which he had bought

with seeds provisions & implements
all were lost
gone down in a coastal squall

had come ahead to secure for them
a place to settle
to lay a claim to lands for those

might never see the shore again
nor speak Spain's unfriendly tongue
nor even their own

seventeen there were
& Lovelace one
had loaned him toward the *Lively's* cost

came not knowing what fortune would hold
in '56 a century later & even more
had come to meet with the Governor

in uniform here to represent
the Council's Neches troops
another river lived along

the photo still retain
taken at the shaking of
Allan Shivers' hand

wearing that brown Explorer tie
with Eagle badge & Beaumont sign
a print shows adolescent shining eyes

could not foresee the how nor why
of a whole life plotted here
as if Estevan had mapped it out

fallen upon by a Comanche band
took the little he had
then gave it back

all but the blankets
his bridle & mainly
his Spanish grammar

crossing the Medina into
the poorest land
he had ever seen

a country vacant of everything
but prickly pear   to him
Laredo the site of perpetual drought

& indolence   traveled on from there
never once inspired
nor Humboldt either not long before

who hoped no other spot on earth
could prove so miserable as what he saw
between Monterrey & Mexico

a judgment shared too by Berlandier
"a lover of solitude
and of picturesque views"

who found its "small
groves of huisache
—whose hairy fruits

make ink as good as gall—
the only ones which even slightly
interrupt the area's monotony"

had encountered no herbaceous plants
but then the Frenchman notes
"despite the apparent barrenness

numerous herds graze nourished by
the thorny nopal . . .
a wagon wheel broken on our first day out"

in '76 traveling there by car
could not compare
for protected by tires from amygdaloids

earlier in '60 had come to play
a wayward erratic part
in Estevan's grandest scheme

his "seminary of learning"
though undreamed of in '56
dressed in that suit of forest green

a poorest excuse for an Explorer Scout
in any event planning then to minister
to pursue the course prescribed

by Reverend Elwood Birkelbach
whose own began
at Jones Prairie & Walker's Creek

with boyhood idols of Buffalo Bill
& a threatened Texas Ranger had hidden there
out in the tall thick chaparral

drafted as chaplain to an island where
"The Purple Shaft" would plow into
the planes parked & loaded there

164 dead from 10 explosions
his own skull torn
when oxygen tanks

blew a concussion would afterwards mean
he would ever stop the communion service
to stuff a Kleenex up his nostril

done he said out of all respect
or would suddenly drip
bright red on the silver plate

this at St. Paul's
Beaumont's South Park Methodist church
where would suffer then a breakdown

sent by the Synod to recover
at a smaller appointment in Rusk
with its famous hospital

handy just in case
serving there his fewer souls
yet could still forget his flock

as his mind sped onward
to a scene envisioned
at a frontier fort

its noonday sun glaring down upon
a dry parade ground from out of the past
inside its stockade a change of guard

when on the tip of an officer's sword
would flash the blinding eye of the Lord
contained & connected all time & space

wanted so to read as he   omnivorously
though too lazy ever to keep the pace
of his devouring each author's volumes

before taking up another's
had said should attend Lon Morris first
then Southwestern above San Gabriel's banks

his alma mater oldest university in State
had heard as he that inner call
for a Methodist man of the cloth

or had thought then was intended to be
though later recalled the sermon
he delivered at evening worship

on a farmer stumbled behind his mule
when up in the sky
spied a big PC

took it as a sign
to go Preach Christ
laid down his reins & answered

but after years of riding circuit
decided to Plow Corn
was all it meant

came likewise instead
to this river street
where a first Poem Cast

here where Barker begins Estevan's trip
never to enter nor ever enroll
in the Perkins Seminary at SMU

Estevan's injunctions long unknown
the trail blazed by Moses overgrown
with believing had already passed beyond

any silly high school history course
one so filled with useless dates
the fiery cloud still up ahead

of the pillars gone before
those would lend instruction in
a poetry struck from desert stone

though even Estevan missed the way
such lines may follow
from Berlandier's road to Monterrey

where huisache made
the writing flow
& now with this backwards glance

retrace that route once more
with its each wrong turn
would come out right

on driving the Volks from Ciudad Victoria
through mountains never ending
the engine straining up one side

breaks whining down the other
around the winding curves
where grinding trucks

hogged those narrow roads
hung miles above
each lush precipitous inviting plunge

each range revealing a higher yet
till reached at last that valley floor
its cacti where the Aztecs saw

their prophesy's wriggling snake
caught in an eagle's beak
& in spite of all as it did for him

that trying year of highs & lows
proved of lasting benefaction
Estevan's own to those may never know

nor ever care how much they owe
beyond any estimate or budget spent
his own limited funds all running dry

sold his watch for food & drink
for posting the latest news to his brother Jim
drawing on Hawkins to tide him over

then ran into an Englishman
loaned him a little more
a General on a mission for

the Chilean state
had fought against its Spanish rule
he an ambassador

perked up at Estevan's Texas plan
even agreeing to split with him
any grant should come his way

& just the same would Wavell share
whatever lands the Texan gained
Arthur Goodall

a guide well-versed in Latin life
his Spanish good
Estevan's improving day by day

wrote to the Congress as best he could
appealed they stay decentralized
not to keep as the Romans had

every province bound to Rome
not to make of its capital city
the nation's single seat & center

when Wavell reminiscing
told of the audacious attack Lord Cochrane staged
his capture of Valdivia's fortress

at the southern port where Cortínez arranged
for my talk on Williams & Spain
in a Spanish even now no match for Estevan's own

there met Carlos' dancer wife   later estranged
& Omar Lara his poet-communist friend
exiled in Rumania after Allende's fall

as was Gonzalo Millán in Montreal
& Oscar Hahn of black rose fame
who had come to this state in '62

he too a part of the same
Chile-Texas exchange
in turn had gone there in '65

returning alone in '66
with María & Darío in '71
Hahn's generation read & followed

translating their lines & lives
those as vines & tendrils kept curling back
to their long thin envisioned land

a tree whose limbs
they would lop but loved
as Hahn who in '73

fled to a salaried job
in Maryland & later the Iowa Workshop
before that Oscar had taught in Arica where

his colleagues all gave welcome
when I lectured in that very same room
where shortly before Vargas Llosa had come

to deliver they said a magisterial speech
though Hahn did not come out
to greet be seen with or hear

a Texan spoke so haltingly
then Ramón Layera to end up here in Austin
with Jo & their kids exposed

to his trial by fire for tenure
rendering Harryette Mullen for Prickly Pear
before that had brought over Lawrence Benford

in Arica led by Ramón & Espagne Pauner
calmly through those thorny fields
of fists & objections the leftists raised

& escorted too by Alicia & Oliver
who excused my use
of imperfect tense & faulty case

& yet by chance would choose
a Chilean expression so dear to all
"to think oneself death in a boat"

got a laugh from their comic phrase
how many later to be herded aboard
sailed off to years of wistfulness

in Oliver's letters the disillusion
from party promises unfulfilled
though he & Alicia never playing the part

the convenient role of refugees
from quote the C.I.A.'s overthrow
taking their lumps in Birmingham

struggling through without complaint
in '71 a turn of events so unforeseen
though in '66 Carlos looking even then

to leave Valdivia's endless rain
its only other season/station the one for trains
its earth damp three hundred sixty-five days

where humid clothing hung to dry
before the oil or paraffin stove
smoked until the windows fogged

his books of Borges' poems
known from then
a friendship formed of all these years

started off from where
Lord Cochrane had led his men
through cannon fired from high above

worked their way through timber & mud
up paths along those sheer rock cliffs
Carlos himself later under the gun

on leaving behind wife & kids
came to scale in Iowan snow
steep bulwarks of the Ph.D.

to storm his way to victory
to win it in himself
the going tough

bogged down by dull demands
delayed by deep affections
pinned him down

the daily need for love
escaped by none
most when far from home

the assault on a foreign front
an endless siege
then came to share

to walk this city's river streets
as had with him where Cochrane won
his visit here a dream come true

to show to him Estevan's setting for
his wished-for language school
& what did he feel

when Wavell spoke
of Carlos'
Andean land

did he see his Colony gazing south
creating bonds as close as these
turning from a deep dependence on

the east with its hold like Rome's
know common views could bridge the gulf
establish a Mediterranean trade & art

on recalling his talk with that British man
now climb once more
Santiago's Cerro Santa Lucía

at the center   at the heart
of María's capital city
& her country too

there where Pedro de Valdivia
battled the Araucano in epic form
there where he founded Santiago

on that eucalyptus-shaded lovers' hill
with its statue of Caupolicán
his bow drawn

his war ending for him
as he sat upon
the Spaniard's sharpened pole

broke & gored his innards
with pain enough
to weep & plead

yet met his death without grimace
his face serene
his eyebrows never twitching

in ecstasy as though
on their wedding bed
until at his feet his Fresia threw

their son had suckled her breasts
child of a captive father
had changed his sex

she severing in shame that sacred knot
Ercilla's history from María's lips
tasted ever after with each caress

carried there to catch & hold her fast
by this river street goes through no more
by an apartment then so overpriced

gone down before
the campus expansion's wrecking ball
two cities   two continents

spliced as one
by a minor composer's major chords
a tuning to that impresario's fervent prose

links from Apennines to Andes
farms since Horace   a plantation near Bolivar
at St. Paul's a minister spread the gospel

his good word pointing the road to read
irked by a poem & stirred to reply
though none has ever quite satisfied

& yet from that beginning
the endless apprenticeship
& in '65 to be selected

as one of fifteen student leaders
among them Ricardo Romo
track-star-historian & all the others

then to find María there
librarian at the binational center
she the more than hoped-for answer

to a life together
on tying her Chilean
with Texan strands

no Graham Sumner loose connection
but an Explorer's
bowline scripture

an unbreakable bond
as indelible as epistolary
musical & river lines

never to unravel
nor knot in a tangle
not ever to slip

Red River

with its sandy land & ruddy undrinkable water
Altus a Texas town till they switched the border
from north to prairie dog of this river's forks
on either side salt cedars with wheat & sorghum
yet living on the other what a difference it made
longing each day for home & a place would swear
had crops superior to those any Okie could grow
caught sore throats from breathing its dusty air
picked up & espoused ever since views so narrow

would make an exception of that Sooner hound
unable to forget or deny Cubby's knowing look
his name mother chose when she volunteered
to take on that rambunctious Cub Scout den
he a part rat terrier wore each badge in turn
wolf lion webelo (bear skipped with a change of age)
sewn on a leather patch & hung from his collar
on hikes wax paper-wrapped for him his half-a-can
swam the Neches twice more than earned his Eagle

survived Houston to whimper under a Beaumont bed
buried by his Hildebrandt Bayou he loved the best
a slough out near Humble Oil's refinery camp
where he chased & barked & dug in holes
after brown swamp rabbits & armadillos
slowly lost his hearing then hit by a car
crawled home to that music room behind the garage
far from his birthplace where in those alien fields
cicadas on mesquites sang & shed their empty shells

with Mom & Dad & brother Tom returned
back across the south fork of this river line
to stay with Granny that first summer there
a week in Fort Worth to cure whatever ailed
has ever been the same outside of this State
in Mexico once more an illness took its toll
while María happy to speak her *lengua* again
to barter in the shops & the open-air stalls
I was laid up for days from just their smells

as Estevan languished in that dingy cell
feverish with dreams of live oak & pecan
with fears his colonists would overreact
saw Butler with horns & a pointed tail
misguiding them all to dissension & war
uncertain if his letters delivered or read
his patience tried if not beyond about as far
as the trials Ben Franklin & Job endured
his prayer one last time to see Peach Point

to be with Mary & sit silent in the shade
of the sweetgum formed a canopy above
in a blend of holly & her sun-dried hair
their thoughts entwining as covering from
the political sun with its nightmare rays
to make it back home & the work to be done
to bring them together & better each one
or forget them & think of himself for a change
o best to recall the snail & its lowly pace

have a local mind from that inextricable time
uprooted at nine by Dad's decision to move
to cross over & sell his Great American Life
to farmers would teach the pulling of bolls
to drive the muddy roads & hook blue catfish
bass with mouths could open big as a fist
then back across to visit with Alvin & Sis
reading on the way of Tom & Huck in a cave
but from any moving car grew nauseous sick

never to make it through those classic books
for a dozen years or maybe was even more
for sure not here in '60 that spring semester
read instead Dickens' *Great Expectations*
Gogol Dostoyevsky & some Latin to boot
sharing then that rat-infested luxurious flat
on Sabine one block east of this river street
where first David Reck & later Jon Bracker
set down in rented rooms their notes or poems

at repainted desks one creating a 12-tone piece
the other his lines on Scholz's bier garten song
those houses now an asphalt sea & live-oak isles
lost for the sake of late models parked on tar

on weekends for the Longhorns' fanatical fans
chanting as defenses shut down Hogs or Frogs
rarely missed a Mustang Bear or Cougar contest
now want them back as a signal caller's errant pass
as on 'Horns' last possession linebacker intercepts

the antique elms removed on Frank Erwin's orders
defied by students had themselves chained to them
despised that Regents Chair with half-lens frames
was he too who killed the Chile-Texas Exchange
Dean Bob King surprised to learn opera his passion
Ron Seeliger mastering Italian listening to the Met
for six Saturdays a year sacked summer's relief
from May to October the green protective leaves
admit with higher rises number of seats increased

for viewing artificial yards in a conference race
with Wally Pryor summing up the play by play
that feeling of a saving tackle a handoff taken
of gaining the first & ten on a third down five
or on a quick opener to pop through & break it
not to turn the ball over on a final critical drive
to suck it up for a last-ditch come-from-behind
snag a sideline toss & tight walk just in bounds
dance into the end zone as the clock runs down

same as Joseph Jones of Waller Creek fame
need trees & plants yet also athletic lessons
a way for Darío to earn some pocket change
by selling in stands his sodas to thirsty fans
for their fraternity flasks of instant courage
as after practicing etudes & Bach partitas
after exercises in math & in chemistry lab
he would await his turn at the back of the line
for the trays of Cokes toted to blasting bands

at half-time their marches to intricate patterns
those formed on the field while staying in step
to memorized tunes practiced morning & night
forming letters & emblems & human designs
performing as they kept each other in mind
all as one to execute their sharp to the rears
pivoting for a diagonal on precisely the spot

re-rehearsing routines & if put down as dull
held up an end belonged had a weight to pull

later on would prefer Rice's chaotic "Mob"
its disorderly helter-skelter in non-uniforms
darting any which way to avoid a semblance
then came together to spell their rival's name
to pay tribute playing an opposing fight song
to the applause for making such fun of it all
yet included too a social or political point
a current comment on a world gone wrong
as crowd consumed nachos & salty popcorn

Estevan's city for memories not these alone
destined as well for the others soon to come
to rent at "The Overlook" odious condominium
erected by "The Shiflet Group" ruined the view
from windows where in July's sweltering heat
could watch the cool bamboo on Poplar Street
one block long yet never remembered as short
in thought from semesters there going on & on
unlike any student account stamped overdrawn

on demand each matching garage apartment
pays the bearer in full from its formative day
with its arch at the foot of a wooden stairway
a set ascending the inner walls of all who are
fruitful though facing a bare treeless yard
still stuccoed white from that unrushed time
when few owned much less could afford a car
walking to classes & for the week's supplies
to Paramount sneak previews Sunday nights

Peyton Place or *Blood and* (wilted) *Roses*
then back to campus through Capitol dome
by way of Elisabet Ney's the leading man
though his coming attractions untaken in
with history never seeming as real as film
a girl's first kiss vampire teeth at her throat
set hearts throbbing not agrarian thoughts
his lines from a letter dated Brasoria 1829
on nothing more than the crop brought in

on Poplar would meet Bracker by accident
in his rented room below & back of garage
a package for him left in that upstairs box
on taking it down had knocked at his door
to be welcomed in to the rest of his life
to his heating plate & his green potatoes
his painting by Klapp of people eating
to long talks with him of Keats & Yeats
listening with him to Mozart & Haydn

in Amarillo would begin his *Penny Poems*
his cards & letters later arriving from Paris
Terre Haute New York or Slippery Rock
San Francisco Hawaii Manila Singapore
in Japan a towering giant ever ill at ease
with his prominent feet & outsized nose
wandering at sea with his extra baggage
of a sister unvisited & mother unwritten
the heaviest load a wife had given up on

would stop by at times but never to tarry
planned once more to start fresh & settle
his poems moving in spite of constraints
to make them pleasant by whatever rules
had painted there his portrait of his father
left it with somebody or other somewhere
made sketches scattered as so many leaves
in '61 had sat for him there in his only chair
then grew morose & withdrew from school

before that having fallen out with George
& once he had moved had roomed alone
when Jon a boon yet injustice everywhere
in despair returned to my Beaumont home
then headed back in June to try it again
to rent with Andy that other twin side
the eastern upstairs with Lloyd below
hefty student joked of his being blind
spent his tuition on a trip to the coast

those carefree days when parents paid
for the learning more outside of classes
than from all those were required to take
appalled by classes failed majors switched

rooms looked to them worse than pig sties
dirty clothes under beds or thrown in closets
weeks of unwashed dishes so fungus-caked
so anguished to understand the finding fault
with truths they acquired much harder ways

in '28 Andy's own folks Margaret & Paul
studied at what then was Texas Wesleyan
its director Reverend Olander Swedish too
in the college co-op both earned their keep
by doing such chores as milking the cows
their fees by cleaning the dormitory house
their teachers themselves students at U.T.
later they too attended & pursued degrees
till quit with Depression to make ends meet

she a maiden Anderson from over by Manor
August her father had styled himself an author
stole time from breadwinning to finish his text
written in his lively & readable patriotic prose
proud to be a *Hyphenated* man as Swenson too
an immigrant citizen tied to his newfound land
& also Sir Swante Palm that collector of books
by those like Charles Darwin considered kooks
neighbors howled when August printed his own

Paul too a second generation but born near Hutto
a little crossing on the wet fork of the San Gabriel
rose three miles wide moved a plumbingless house
his blacksmith father told the story & "as it goes
when none could settle on a name for the town
one Swede had spoken up 'guess we gotta Jonah'
and it stuck"   regaled too with slow endless tales
of putting in a sulfur plant in a Wyoming snowstorm
"well now you might say it weren't exactly no snap"

nor was it then to explain to a friend
or write a poem meant what was meant
much less find the girl would last forever
ask Andy who thought for certain he did
a redhead from Lamesa had led him on
& how many others to feel it wasn't worth it

when always the words just came out wrong
in Batts Hall inspired by the native speakers
but on exams their accents made no sense at all

in Latin had James Hitt & Christian Smith
have never gotten over having ever let go
of their dead language they offered alive
after convoluted Cicero had then arrived
at *The Aeneid* abandoned after one canto
a voyage only known in verse translation
that ur-journey missed in Garrison Hall
with its wooden desks such tested ships
by passages ventured on Mare Nostrum

o Estevan would not have been pleased
but then he was never to stand in that line
march back & forth at the Varsity Theater
in the movement had its beginning in 1960
for integration of every off-campus movie
seemed harmless enough at the local "Y"
taking part in meetings held by the SDS
nailing picket signs at the Methodist Center
then holding them up to be taunted & jeered

hurt most by voices from the back of a bus
yelled they didn't need no white boys' help
as if to get even with him in a Mexican jail
had gone to fulfill Moses' colonial dream
those just out to spite whomever they saw
unaware & unconcerned he had gotten off
on figuring it out later so hard to swallow
could not have then since had not yet seen
the book where Barker had set it all down

knew only those rooms he had lectured in
in Garrison on declining Hitt's declensions
or sat in the Old Library named for Eugene
beneath its high beams with stars & angles
reading for the classes that spring semester
the serial novels in pairs assigned by Cline
Russian & Victorian courses taken together
falling asleep in plush brown leather chairs
as lamps cast a soft light on words & floors

reached by marble stairs splotched with gray
a stone in use below for those urinals too
the men's with brown-stained wooden doors
one's knifed & dated plea "Susan I need you"
& how did he ever expect her to find it there
even to have heard his biographer's lectures
would that have aided in making it through
to have had that professor of history explain
how such crises have come & will again

to have listened to him in Houston say
to that audience how "Recurrent doubts
are a wholesome antidote to complacency"
would that have made a difference then
when everything led to a pointless end
unlikely unless it might have dawned
Estevan's very own "Chief" Eugene
had a mind from Riverside & Palestine
though even Christian restored no faith

dropped Mister Enthusiasm's epic class
true epithet for an Aeneas who ever came
armed with anecdotes for all the fates
who had hiked & blocked at Temple High
like Entellus had put on Herculean gloves
but a sense of humor his knockout punch
& after a tennis match or leveling a house
would lift his flute with enormous hands
to balance it at his lips & render an etude

yet would not sit still for listening to Liszt
music of the unwashed with all their kitsch
like Ez rejected loans of a usurious system
ever longed to erect a rammed-earth home
undaunted by a strikeout in the game of love
a friend still in deed to his three ex-spouses
did light or heavy repairs around their houses
on visits the kids sleeping crammed among
his Greek & Latin texts those Loeb classics

had Estevan gone back east had any cared
for certain not those who criticized most
their constant resentment reason enough

to have left the reins in ungrateful laps
returned & left them to fend for themselves

always there are others to take one's place
what any man does can be done by another
where then is the honor in suffering through
why bother if fault is found with even the best
& in time a dozen at least may do it better

though none can deny the performance given
in success or failure the learning still earned
never to be taken away nor ever replaced
better be blamed than remain unchanged
from fear too little or too much be said

one student argued against being included
in *Bernie Feldman's Detective Cookbook*
said it would only be thrown in the trash
who never turned in a single assignment
to do or not to do the eternal clash

& if not fated it still seems wholly needful
to descend in indecision to some nether world
to stumble there through each bubbling fosse
for the knowing all those have gone before
their works awaiting whoever would follow

when Webb too met with hopeless moments
would hold up the image of William E. Hinds
& think on the books his benefactor sent him
"However much I was tempted to quit
I could not quit without letting him down"

even before the first issue of *Riata* was out
the announced East-West theme under attack
a satirical letter published in the deadly *Texan*
a new cause for thinking would give it all up
when resigning had meant never meeting Jim

no trips to Printing Division on this river street
to approve the plate & later to punch the holes
showed in the center of his blind embossing
with a rice-paper sheet's burnt-orange smear
reviewed by Ambrose as a collector's item

not to discover Zanders' "Fugue for an Island"
John's story rejected by *New Campus Writing*
then accepted as edited with the title changed
with Jim hired by Printing as a book designer
if not for himself went on for Mary & Moses

but what to do with a disparaging Frantz
has seen Barker's *Life* as far too partial
or with Santa Anna's remark in Castañeda
that Estevan employed an English guile
to trick a generous Mexican nation

can contradict nothing answering the charge
had gathered the material as any despot would
had made the student magazine too prettified
choose rather to re-remember Ransom's call
to come see him at his Chancellor's Office

on his pile carpet before his mahogany desk
stood in awe as he said of that autumn issue
reminded him of *Texas Quarterly* model of all
on its editorial staff he would offer a position
though the necessary funds never came through

while he spent instead the obscene figures
acquiring the works of the dead & buried
authors from Britain France anywhere but here
ignoring there on Rio Grande a Hickey at work
on stories never to grace its expensive pages

ten years later left it for Hudspeth to run
even earlier had started its downhill slide
from halcyon days held Zukofsky & Dickey
with Kim Taylor illustrating their latest lines
then fallen to a versifying of the safest type

in the Tower saw Frances with her aerial view
chain smoking there in her masculine shoes
approached her naively to edit for free
return its past glory helping solicit the new
had no patience she said with the contemporary

blamed her alone for no poem getting in
María declared it an obsession with print
lusting after another still bolder by-line
in Dante's age if not cardinal a venial sin
she they say kept academy out of the red

& after all the badmouthing thought & said
let in when Don Miguel requested a review
that omnibus coming out as "Who's Afraid
of the Big Bad Poem?" to feel an absolute fool
yet not at Ransom's behest so never the same

though later on when Bass would up & resign
leave Harry's "center of our cultural compass"
Ransom fulfilled his word in a roundabout way
through revelations gained in on-the-job training
from letters & photos his hoarding had saved

next to Woolworth's at Dacy's Congress St. store
never minded running fill-ins to that dusty stock
yet rather than shelving those slings & pumps
could take down from PRs a blue-covered *Ulysses*
in PQs Emerson's trenchant thoughts on Alighieri

find inspiring quotes in Harry's frontier essays
with immigrant marks notched not on firearms
but in journal jottings by doctors & bookworms
Swante Palm Ashbel Smith & Sherman Goodwin:
self-examination is "duty insurance" counters sin

forever indebted & if again repaid too late
yet enter in accounts his bringing together
of the manuscript drafts & priceless proofs
as Estevan acted on each stranger's behalf
risked wreckage as well for those to come

two magnets attracted plowman & scholar
& despite the fact of living a century apart
linked in the mind as this river's two forks
by the profit ever from the prophetic force
of their cargoes' hopeful forward thoughts

San Jacinto

down steps on Memorial Museum's western side
Proctor's sculpted rearing mustangs symbolize
"seas of pristine grass   men riding free"
those borne on their bare or saddled backs
carried without the ruinous cost of oil & gas

explorers braves & cowhands plunge ahead
on Estevan's '29 map whole herds filling up
the vacant tracks before the searing brands
of excessive horse sense broke their spirits
all gone with trails to Alberta & Cheyenne

while a block south in Memorial Stadium
Longhorns now dig in for a goal-line stand
showing what it takes to come from behind
proving on another crisp autumn afternoon
how on being down one can turn it around

always this street conjures that historic place
where at siesta time between the silken sheets
Yellow Rose would give herself for a 36th state
Sam surprising tented "Napoleon of the West"
then opposed Austin as governor & capital seat

yet none of that had mattered to Joseph Jones
the vituperative troll on his noonday rounds
picked from Waller Creek unsightly plastic
attacked through inventories in poetic prose
those who cast it from sidewalk or bridge

for this city's drainage said more to him
than any points scored at a championship
& the only battle he found worthy to fit
not one pitched at a bayou-headed river
but the struggle to save his campus crick

riffles beside shuttle bus & faculty traffic
as it meanders along with this river street
from museum & stadium to Santa Rita's rig
then one fork flows toward Centennial Park
by the Drum & in sight of Hamilton Home

the other continuing toward Scholz's Garten
past pink office buildings of polished granite
the State Library with its anonymous portrait
of Estevan in oil on a window-shade canvas
to Service on 5th typeset Joe's *Life on Waller*

his chapters written on near half-a-century
of sack lunching to delicate or raucous calls
from purling water's to wading grackle's
as he observed the ghostly crawfish scuttle
& gathered in the high-carat sunfish gold

counting his riches in the moss's green
as it clung to a slab of fossilized stone
found it too in cypress trees' fallen finery
patterns dropped unseen by pecan & oak
sewing their patchwork of light & shadow

first came here in that '60 spring semester
to read in the middle of Joseph's stream
Vanity Fair & alternately *War & Peace*
stretched at length on smooth limestone
with its soothing eddies about & beneath

confused as to characters in which ballroom
with their uninvented war one & the same
unaware of "an old codger" waged his own
against the University's landscape machine
would narrow its lovely water-carved bed

pour concrete on banks & bulldoze its figs
if those to come back as did Bobby Layne
others of its sylvan ancestors unseen again
luscious leaves lost from limbs of trunks
the subject of the troll's outraged lament

his infernal fight making such total sense
his defense of even the lowliest weeds
lobbied to make his creek a garden park
with two gauging stations a record complete
a unique model for the nation to monitor

feared for his city named at first Waterloo
its rill to suffer defeat from dumped refuse

or at the hands of careless mindless planners
neo-Bonapartes mapping outlandish growth
a building blitz to overrun its weak position

yet how ban the trashers from Estevan's Eden
generations brought up among cactus & sand
or Elisa from joining in a Tchaikovsky dance
not 1812 cannon but *Nutcracker*'s yule ballet
at the PAC within earshot of Jessen Cascade

where among the string section Darío played
the Brandenburg 6th & Musorgski's *Mountain*
María searched authority files at Public Affairs
& at the HRC raised out of turbulence & haste
able at last to make use of my terminal degree

across from Proctor's statued mustang band
wisterias still twine around their metal posts
their pungent clusters draped as bluish grapes
blooming through each enrollment stampede
& would ever bend towards having them both

a low score on GRE had meant neither one
had it not been for insisting for half an hour
to be given a chance by Acting Dean Hughes
to prove through probation could do the work
was not he said material for graduate school

in Battle Hall sat on its forbidding first floor
above his office the library named for Barker
wasn't about to accept any raven's Nevermore
had denied access to Estevan's archival bequest
to editorship of *Riata* & being chosen for Chile

to find María there at her binational center
an unsecured loan would make it all happen
taken out through John Lomax's Texas Exes
then returned to fragrant Batts Hall unforgotten
to form a part of non-tenured instructors "pool"

each semester just before or after classes began
to have a low-paid temporary contract renewed
a fortune from having been in '64 barely let in

& able in '76 to make that class's assignment
to write their poems seated beside its stream

walked from Parlin Hall across East Mall
to the bridge back of Etter's Alumni Center
where John Lang Sinclair's pep song hangs
on brown butcher paper in his fading hand
passing with students the site of old B Hall

gone before summer '61 when had sat on grass
watching movies shown at Waggener & in '62
not to cram for that exam on Arab Nationalism
past labs of E.P. Schoch founded Longhorn band
by ROTC flag then descended the fountain stairs

through windblown spray from its jetted waters
spilling transparent in view of B. Iden's Theater
named for Payne told Ray who took his course
when he roomed with Andy how Olivier's eyes
look all but dead   see it mostly in his *Hamlet*

Andy at the time into Igor's classical *Symphony
in C* & *Rake's Progress* set to Auden's libretto
Fantasticks longest running off-Broadway show
in it Tom Jones parodies that Professor lovingly
an ex-student learned from him as did Rip Torn

in '67 saw him in *Beach Red* with Cornel Wilde
another bloody war film on another Pacific Isle
till the Japs a father & son turned suddenly real
snipers in the infested jungles fighting with fear
as righteous invading Marines close in for a kill

saw in the same movie house industrial waste
emptied on the screen & staining the river pink
Perkins in *Pretty Poison* disturbed at his best
a Hobbs picture show only a handful attended
where in a *Volpone* scene María's labor began

brings back again that walk down fountain steps
to the turnaround bridge spans Waller's banks
with that writing class there to watch & listen
remember Arnie Cheryl Peggy Jules & Gene
like them would compose from whatever came

a piece on Wukasch mover of Symphony Square
on its stage beside Joe's creek Darío would play
as it rippled between his trio & those would hear
while up the street & stream on another occasion
lunched with Joe & Lord Byron his gimpy friend

a grackle hobbled but with beak held high
claiming territorial rights in spite of his limp
his feeder with khaki cap & a bag with straps
for collecting the discarded new & old artifacts
his glasses agleam with Waller's reflected light

through willows & vines had climbed with him
clambering over the cypress trees' knobby knees
as he inveighed against racket of cars & mowers
needless motors   men mad for bronzed Bevos
he who had read Neruda seated on Incan stones

who in '44 had founded *The Library Chronicle*
later taken over by Dr. Maurer a veritable savior
made it possible to follow them both at the HRC
as trimmer of that quarterly's display window
its treasures shown through Caledonia & color

its scraps deposited in this B-Western desert
by the Brits & Frogs had grown so incensed
after laughing their ways to Savings & Loan
forgetting their Elgin marble & Rosetta stone
with legacies GTT to find the joke on them

can still resent taxes Ransom siphoned there
or so it seemed then & even now can appear
on his leaving so little for the alive & active
artwork worthy of public & private support
yet could not detract from satisfaction taken

in working with scholars who sent from afar
their posted articles or with a local like Slate
unraveled the screenplay by Reisman & Zuk
Ulysses from '32 with Louis 5 years into "A"
like nightfall Joseph wove it with not a quote

in a '77 class had Ted a bright student cellist
heard & wrote on the concert of Mahler's 5th

had Clare Colquitt then as teaching assistant
her essay printed in '84 on *Contempo*'s years
in '85 on Edith Wharton's letters to *cher ami*

at Duke had met & married Bradford Mudge
who in '83 had contributed his special piece
on Sara Coleridge with her Spanish & Greek
on her editing of her father's difficult texts
on her bout with the family's poppy disease

Irene Rostagno on Knopf & its Latin boom
Carpentier *Lost Steps* Donoso *Obscene Bird*
novels & stories from Amazonian backlands
all tracked by her through the files & reviews
ins & outs of the careers of Alfred & Blanche

Rick Lawn on Ross Russell's KC-styled jazz
on his Dial contracts with Bird & Schoenberg
& had coaxed Gene Ramey out of retirement
born in '13 beside Waller at Red River & 14th
bassist in on bebop birth with Parker & Monk

Christensen unearthing Olson's song of Worms
in a dark passage of Dahlberg's correspondence
found it slogging his "squalid marshes of wrath"
in "dungy sheepcotes" bitten by his Sodom fleas
then the "dreary impasse" as bottom-dog friends

differing as if a chorus of Edward & Charles
he an Aggie with lines emanating from Bryan
a promoter of Texas poetry on his radio show
featuring so many from McDonald to Burford
a Beat Snyder too & Black Mountain Creeley

branded a provincial elitist & charged with bias
on leaving Paul out of that '81 bilingual edition
Cow's Skull a collection of mostly native poets
had excluded him when included other émigrés
who had done for the State poetry so much less

Estevan preferred families over unmarried men
longsuffering not drifters at harvest & roundup
discouraged riffraff not the industrious debtors

where else go for working off a farm had failed
no first-come first-served basis nor room for all

King denied tenure with three books to his credit
his essays better than enemies would ever admit
on Ezra's library   his triangle with Hilda & Bill
Michael's rich digs for others in Ransom's "theft"
gave release too from tedium of making a living

& with Tom Zigal having the privilege conferred
of catching & marking typos in galleys & proofs
checking blue lines & correcting footnote or head
regional surveys contributed to his *Pawn Review*
meeting with Luis to discuss *La calavera* & Perú

would've been deprived of Sunder's vital course
on Cabeza de Vaca Catlin & Bancroft's Villagrá
Webb's sixshooter & bobwire & windmill plains
Black cowboys & dogfaces had opened the range
native peoples in W.W. Newcomb driven extinct

yet survive in his book on diets of larva & feces
corn & communal hunting & running down deer
from Ice Age to the white man's colder coming
in his writings on the artists Kirkland & Petri
the two warm exceptions with brushes & pens

like a watercolor & pencil Randall repaired
with the aid of Conservation's fabulous lab
so vicarious so vivid in a way only Petri had
with a black boy on horseback turned to look
at a keg of water pulled as a white boy rides

as he holds in his one hand a wooden bucket
passing into cactus from the moss-hung trees
in the background a bonneted mounted figure
races off at breakneck speed as a female black
a basket on her head is left to bring up the rear

the Mescalero pictographs Forrest had drafted
from a rock art painted in a Hueco Tanks cave
symbols he drew to save from graffiti & flood
Newcomb would revive & have them printed
from his pages to Inshallah home of Jim Smith

at 43rd & Waller its tradition of hosting the arts
where arrowheads still mark their sacred camps
Elisa invited there to shine at her first cast party
from Comanche flints to a daughter in leotards
to the earlier roles played by Bugbee & Barker

said he didn't know why he would even bother
but go on over then to English & see Dr. Crow
said it would do no good   he could only agree
so next-door to Parlin to that graduate advisor
where informed at the Office Crow wasn't in

then sent to Dr. Maurer his assistant instead
on knocking greeted by his billy-goat voice
a gruff Come in called through opaque glass
at his desk Oscar just barely lifting his head
peered into a drawer he would open & close

on hearing of Hughes & then of Crow not in
looked hard at the drawer & closed it again
would spot in the pause on one of his walls
the copy of a print by Jon Bracker's friend
Frank Stack etching of a garage apartment

spoke of that & of first meeting Jon in 1960
edited *The Ranger* in its heyday   How is he
in some way from there would bring up jazz
his favorites by far James P. Johnson & Fats
another Waller than one paraphrased by Ez

after digressions intriguing as his Trollope's
as he'd stare at his hands pushing & pulling
he came at last to ask but without looking up
what was needed & hearing a permit to enter
jotted one down & gave it his face still awry

caught on the other's surprise & displeasure
as he glared at that note with Maurer's okay
a victory impossible with cut-offs & quotas
rents beyond any lower middle-class means
& more so with grades just mediocre at best

to have missed it all by that computed score
but admit the Dean never slammed the door

though then & there thought it hardly a crack
yet over the long haul opened the floodgates
as Oscar's note delivered the rivers & streets

the visions & verses of the houses & halls
meditations on Waller where Joe patrolled
found him alone there still clearing debris
fallen trees & the sewage all backing it up
forming foul gray stands of polluted scum

even as the Committee of full professors
would dam the way for the grant or raise
& fire the instructors had carried the load
or those like King had proven their worth
one professor rummaging in disposal bins

in his briefcase his smashed aluminum cans
not so much for recycling as to cash them in
another in nifty tennis togs & shoes to match
ever ready during office hours for a set or two
Joseph only at Waller lunchtime or weekend

cleaning the creek that it move & glisten
preserved its creatures for future viewers
for reading of literatures from far & near
taught World English till mandatory age
his lectures teaching a language of flow

let another codger come if only just one
for it takes but a single life vs. the litter
another pupil like him of finest teachers
those like Heraclitus Walton & Thoreau
proffer to the present the lessons live on

for Joe a steward of the wisdom in water
who drew too from its deeps & shallows
a slaking drink of local & distant cultures
ever taking its history as a rod to measure
the insatiable need for fuel & horsepower

Nueces

was this the street where Donnie stayed
favorite of granny Polk on daddy's side
who dropped off his date near Forest Park
slid on a wet curve lost control & died
Tommy after delivering his Green Berets
flipped & crushed under the steering wheel
that cousin first & then that only brother

on coming in '56 those losses still remote
later in decade to find this city a sanctuary
one flown to year-round by migrating minds
with its environment conducive to idea & art
but found Donnie's fraternity in mourning then
for a member died in a wreck the night before
his wake held on Lavaca at the Scottish Rite

its windowless walls as mysterious as death
walked past them from downtown to campus
after arriving that first trip by Greyhound bus
a representative then for Boy Scouts Week
put up at Bergstrom in the Air Base barracks
attended a Union ball where Sinclair's "Eyes"
still peer across West Mall to Architecture

stood looking on as the cute couples danced
thrilled to be a part though ever at a distance
if future times & friends not dimly perceived
felt nonetheless somehow this city's heartbeat
the wonder of those Commons looming ahead
to gather there for hearing with Hickey's circle
his pronouncements so outrageous & o so subtle

there in '62 Franklin Haar going over his poems
typed with inkless ribbons on coffee-stained sheets
in '77 caught with a class phrases for *The Poet Trap*
"heavy with Hamburger fog" "rehearsals downbeats"
those of Laura & Renee on listening to a brass quintet
playing where Shirley Bird Perry had Jesson engrave
emblems in limestone above its expanded entrance

to longhorn mocker jack rabbit & cactus
horned frog & owl a prairie dog & rattler
added rook & knight masks comic & tragic
harp & lute along with quill brush & palette
festive grapes an opened text a swaying nude
all embraced among learning's leaves & fruit
but then it may not have even been Nueces

& yet that first day still distinctly comes in
to Webb his clear as "pictures on a screen"
but set to record three unforgettable precepts
left on his typewritten page an unfilled space
have located two vacant lots two blocks apart
one for certain right where Walter first lived
when from MK&T he took a streetcar north

on the other a frat house the city condemned
razed in later years after its members hazed
even kicked & pissed on a passing student
would that have been that cousin's then
Webb as a frosh in on a sophomore's shooting
a fight in '12 brought passage of a hazing law
but failed to save a Corps cadet dead in '84

each on a corner   the Greeks' at 24th
Walter's at 22nd two such distant worlds
the former's brick now reduced to rubble
but thanks to all John Morris's trouble
the latter transported to a garbage heap
where goats then grazed on native grass
with windows in view of Balcones Fault

& whose if not of one & all
have failed to read or ever to right
past or present for the future's sake
will leave it for a John to sacrifice
so one may know where Webb first wrote
recalls how across & down this river street
Bugbee came to rescue Estevan's repute

its panels of a history of tongue & groove
of "pumpkin" pine made tung-oil smooth
porcelain knobs on doors of a perfect fit
in '80 before Webb would room & board

kids by height had scribbled their arithmetic
on Miss M.V. Jones's Select School walls
early solutions for any would double-check

those recovered by John's detective love
as too Pompee's fine hand-slotted frame
wheelwright's 1875 German-French design
remodeled & added to circa 1880 or '79
to preserve it John to lose wife & daughter
Anne preferring IBM & the corporate gains
from her had first learned a bit of Russian

would lead to shores of Pushkin's poem
with its bronze horseman & stately Neva
grown restless with wind & a backing sea
until on its rising it drives a wedge of water
between Yevgeny   bedridden invalid tosses
& turns   & Parasha   his dearly beloved
John's restoration become a Nueces in flood

such pain of separation relieved on spraying
his Wright's pavonia an endangered species
watched as garden stones darkened with wet
the bacon & alibates flint lightening the day
dogtooth jasper chalcedony calcite crystals
copper cedar roots strips of petrified wood
varieties of cactus all experts on survival

his own spirits lifted on dampening those
on observing the colonies of lichen thrive
the patient decades it took them to build
their green encampments on barren fields
plowed under by developers in an afternoon
forced again to move his matrimonial house
by those would profit from his secluded home

odyssey of the place where Webb composed
country boy wrought up by the magic meaning
of words set down in their orderly rhythm
with a music for those then & those to come
though a writing course did not recommend
just wide reading bridge building hoboing poker
well-drilling lovemaking wind jamming & war

John a model in that historian's mold
reared on the range up near Amarillo
from here to Houston drove moving vans
like Terry Raines the native printer
had done it himself whatever it was
John's Russian major "oh it's nothing much"
Terry's geodesic dome "anyone could have"

such unassuming manners o so sicken
how ever hope even to master English
any mechanical failure can hardly fix
those salvage resurrect repair & restore
Terry reusing scrap for his outside stairs
joists from a demolished university roof
iron from Seton   he Brackenridge born

who grants to things a second chance
will allow an elevator door to rise again
the rejected pillars to support once more
he exploring a Texan or a Mexican cave
the cool of his own deep modest ways
while John underneath a newer veneer
discovers a truer color & a house's date

Terry in his stand of oak & cedar
on one side of a grassy arroyo bed
just off the Kyle to Wimberley road
constructed a bunk & woodstove cabin
facing a tree-topped limestone ledge
its bathroom put in without a door
left open to creek & passing deer

from lumber & a telephone pole
he built it first with its lighted path
leads to where the print shop's now
to a pond dammed up & rocked about
stocked with ducks & sodded around
from a sturdy trunk ran a cable down
to slide from slope to a refreshing splash

had only begun just beyond the rise
a two-storey house of his own design
its shell to become his & Suzy's home
living meanwhile atop his circular shop

out a windowed room above the grove
views its changing leaf tones come & go
he at sundown reading or at the piano

in work boots & his plaid flannel shirt
his cap on above his sun-tanned face
with nicked glued & ink-stained hands
plays Bach inventions on a baby grand
between his Heidelberg two-color runs
& burning of plates for an overdue job
collating & binding & trimming it out

so exasperating with his constant delays
at midnight Jim redoing a dummy again
re-moving the head & re-spacing a line
waited on both with a shortened fuse
shooting off before recoil of remorse
knowing this pair got the poetry read
a layout & printing to match the muse

the two in doing so paying the price
or kids & ex-wives bearing the cost
a son ever uncertain to whom to turn
for years not touching nutritious food
would eat no veggies no salad nor fruit
dropped out of schools public or private
tried this tried that friendless & confused

with fresh spring or cool fall mornings
daughters born before the oval bedroom
waking to another stranger sleeping over
to mothers cooking meals in a rusting bus
still parked within sight of a latest live-in
summers split between parental dreams
immolation on altars of idyllic communes

though Bugbee & Estevan knew none of this
for Lester no marital but misery of Fort Bliss
having tied no knot just stuck to his books
balanced the accounts & wrote them down
for those thereafter would inherit the land
or those later on would wish to discover
who tilled it first   who ran with the ball

saved newspaper clippings & cut out ads
collected a flyer with Rootatorial cheers
recorded the Longhorns' clever dodging
when 'Varsity boys laid it on Houston's ten
knocked their whole line into smithereens
with Bethea scoring behind that Texas wall
though "Wortham failed on every easy goal"

when gowns cooperated with citizens of town
& a fullback sang in the University Quartette
the program included a violin & mandolin trio
Bugbee even retaining their sheet music parts
from Hancock Opera House a *Ben-Hur* handout
two photos of Walt Whitman at ages 53 & 68
one of Gladstone gave Lester his middle name

even preserved Dr. Dayton's doggerel song
"The first of the villains who came to this state
Was runaway Stephen F. Austin the great!"
made deeply sad by good intentions of friends
tarred & feathered men in the leader's absence
of his Colony's first two years Bugbee notes
just one case of theft not a single homicide

& would register the amount Estevan asked
for his services to colonists in want of cash
willing to take any property not "a dead loss"
horses mules cattle furs peltry beeswax hogs
dressed deer skins or homemade cloth
"will sacrifice my own interest rather
than distress them for one red cent"

out of his own pocket paid a draftsman
to plot the tract each deed called for
"The great expenses voluntarily incurred
must forever free him from the charge
sounds like sarcasm to speak of defrauding
'shook off the Yoke and dispersed the cloud
had so long kept his settlers in the dark"

"Bugbee from even slenderer means
advanced money for labor and postage
to solicit *Quarterly* members by mail"
"grew to manhood in Johnson County

the post oak & black jacks of Cross Timbers
on the southwest fringed by the Brazos River"
"1890-91 lived at 2110 August St. now Nueces"

only "avoidable expense" his occasional trip
to visit the theatre to catch a Salvini
an Irving Terry in *Merchant of Venice*
his family concerned he had joined a fraternity
his mother sending extra money now & again
never telling the father who was so far in debt
"made 18 bales but won't come out much ahead"

like Webb went off later for the advanced degree
Walter never wanted to leave & said he believed
to have stayed in state had been much better off
a silly superstition to him such going away
said Oxford & Cambridge great from being inbred
on the train home after he had flunked his doctoral
luxuriated in a soft Texas voice's welcome drawl

at Columbia Bugbee worked his way with ease
through the academic details massed to impede
but physicians' bills & the chronic school fees
his dear mother's death & his efforts to lessen
his sister's monotonous days back on the farm
forced his return before he had made it through
here to a pitiful salary with his time running out

always his classes prepared with exhaustive care
would never lecture but move from desk to desk
questioning & discussing each student's response
after the bell all would gather about him for more
taking precious minutes from his unfinished Life
one recalled his winding & rewinding the chain
of a watch had gone ticking relentlessly amain

"In looking back I know now that over
and over again Bugbee's sound judgment
his knowledge of human nature   patient
and persistent insistence
that young men may be led
but not driven
saved from disaster the B Hall experiment"

his allotment of a mere six active years
ended as the century turned to nineteen-one
in Woodbury near Hillsboro his studies began
having taken part there in various debates: Resolved
That woman has more influence over man than money
"walked to Pleasant Point for the mail and received
a searching letter from DAISY declaring our friendship over"

That the white man has a better right to the States
than the Indian   That works of art are more attractive
to the eye than nature   at Mansfield College
wrote "Queer Queries":   What is the "River of Blood"?
Ans. Colorado:—signifying "bloody water"
from Horace copied how none's content with his own occupation
yet no one will exchange positions with another

had entered the University January 1887
family resources stretched for the second semester
"along the line took an introductory course in the language
he was to use most in his subsequent investigations"
Spanish discouraged in the '60s the choice German or French
declared no important literature written in it since Cervantes
yet in February '65 to discover Parra's antipoems in *Motive*

a vein opened up through the Undergraduate periodicals room
another lodestone would draw towards what richness to come
under classical quotations at Main symbolled rafters at Barker
to read there the lines & stanzas & to take passage once more
sinking in seats & hearing that antipoetry ring true
moments placed in settings let them happen over & over
secret mine shafts revealed   when & where the clue

pulled later to Alonso Ercilla Blest Gana & Pezoa Véliz
Huidobro Mistral Neruda & Lihn   then on to Cuba
& the three trapped tigers of Cabrera Infante
Carpentier's enlightenment   Lezama Lima's paradiso
García Márquez's Macondo   Mexico's Rulfo Pacheco & Paz
the Tiresias affair in Borges   Sábato Puig & Cortázar
the Marios in Montevideo   Vargas Llosa's green house in Perú

in San Felipe Estevan had established first
instruction in English but of prime importance
the teaching of other of the modern tongues
"and especially of Spanish"   from a cholera attack

would not recover   gone by the end of 1836
in March '35 had written under the clouds of war
to tell Perry to "keep the children in school"

debunked by John Henry Faulk on public TV
as first real estate agent offered the others' lands
on lowest terms   as the world turns
Estevan's demeanor taking on a look so sinister & cubist
his cross-eyed view of the darker as a barbaric race
"the enemy prepared to enlist the Negroes free or slave"
a serious threat to the peerless civilized white

statements made as his health & patience gave way
but to Faulk just another enterprising racist
his passport to a promised land stamped nil & void
more a Moses forbidden entrance than his father before
reduced to a writer of ads & clever commercials
adept at attracting & luring as in later years
the high-tech biz of Silicon Valley & MCI

in defense think quickly of athletic John Seals
linebacker offensive guard & philosophy major
on the first team recruited by Darrell Royal
had run wind sprints with a fractured fibula
now pediatric neurologist reads Johnson & Blake
in '60 wearing his jersey to Silber's Plan II class
knowing full well that Dean abhorred the sport

Bugbee a booster both of the jocks & poets
close associate of Ed Blount & Hans Hertzberg
two "completely Bohemian in taste & conduct"
Blount later a dermatologist never happy he said
except in some dream-world creating his poems
French imitations or based them on Grecian stones
filled them with nightingales he had never seen once

took imagery from most anywhere but his Hillsboro home
never from this city   not even U.T.'s Forty Acres
the closest an Arkansas scene from his passing train
yet Bugbee would send his verses to publishing firms
in between the History I & II exams he gave each term
"After 350 A.D. to what provincial official would an order
to organize an expedition against the Picts be addressed?"

Hertzberg's "Would-Be Epic" *Lawyers and Laurels*
subtitled "Didactic History of the Junior Law Class"
printed here in 1891 by Eugene Von Boeckmann
more the sort of thing Bugbee must have wanted to read
who wrote for young men & women not to by-pass
their own University for some out-of-state college
"From every point of view this is undesirable

prevents the youths from becoming thoroughly imbued
with ideals obtaining" in their own backyards
"becoming thoroughly acquainted with resources
interests and the people of their own community"
must have cherished Hans's use of place names
a town or city for each classmate's special quality
"Young oak from Oakland a pine tall Tyler son of toil

Smith of Fort Worth fond of Tennis & Tennyson
makes much of racket & ball
but's sometimes silent in the Junior Hall"
those who tow the law & toe the waltz equally
"May they cut in life's quadrilles capers gracefully"
the short of stature but stentorian tongued
those at first come in low but finish on the highest rung

"Thro' meadows brooks in placid clearness flow
Without wild roaring or tempestuous show
So does our Junior Brooks' balanced brain
Work steady on
And 'shyster lawyer' will never soil his name"
of himself the poet will only say "am not thus vain
As to speak self while better men remain

The harp strings break in twain—
Ne'er will they breathe such melody again!
Ne'er was a theme so genial to my heart
Ne'er was it so hard from any theme to part"
then left it all for the Windy City
fell down an elevator shaft "grievously crippled"
his *Century* rejection slip the final crushing blow

Hans' *Lyrics of Love* a "poetaster's ill-tuned lyre"
while Bugbee changed the tone of historical writing
visited Colonel Bryan owned Estevan's archive
"stored in a tower room at his home in Quintana

to protect [it] from inundation by Gulf storms
more precious to him than a heritage of gold"
made headway on the Life then had to give it up

Barker convinced it would have been brilliant
but had to travel to Junction for his failing health
his case diagnosed at Fort Bliss as tuberculosis
prescribed "rigorous exercise" as suitable care
"Despite their high appreciation of his services
the regents had no power to continue his [pay]
and the tragic pity was that he needed" it so

"I am living a pretty hard life in El Paso
In Austin I at least deluded myself
into thinking that I passed for *somebody*
bank presidents would bow cordially
freshmen tip their hats   girls beam beamingly
but now as I pass along I hear
there goes another lunger   need a city ordinance

to keep them away   Have been packing grapes
with a family near Isleta   made with Dr. Baird
microscopic examinations   miss the classes
research on the Colony   can't imagine the University
on opening day   to be there when it starts
but to take no part"   at banks of the Rio Grande
on March 17 1902   dead two months shy of 33

his hero of pneumonia at 43
in a December cold in his unheated shack
that last month there would belatedly draft
his proclamation against the slavery trade
but the damage done & then Bugbee gone
had just begun to save his rightful place
many with longer lives with less to show

most with regrets for their wasted days
the owed unpaid a love left unexpressed
points of unsettled arguments unrecalled
some with no heirs to follow in their steps
others with offspring would later question
stands not taken or reject those that were
all they long stood for & abided to bring

must await another to gird on the sword
who will seek in truth no revenge of time
come rather to recover the candid words
to copy documents & set records straight
both those written & the ways they lived
if self-justified yet needful & deserving of
a Barker born *en buena hora   un mío Cid*

from *KD: a Jazz Biography*

Prophesying

if a steady gig gathers moss it sets the food
on dinner plates & lowers the marital stress
K would keep his vows & a music mistress
too & he kept them both in a mellow mood

then parts ways with Art did he not foresee
indulging a craving to form & lead his own
quintet would risk ending up a rolling stone
was it in the cards or had Ken chosen to be

even before he left led a '55 Blue Note date
Afro-Cuban of March 29th his then ten-inch
with his three fine originals seemed a cinch
to make it as a leader his trumpet solo great

on his "Minor's Holiday" Grieg's "Anitra's
Dance" lifting him to new daring new drive
Potato's conga elevates too & if "Afrodisia"
a letdown "Basheer's Dream" coming alive

K on top Cecil's baritone touching bottom
with Mobe's reed tasting of a cigar & rum
J.J.'s trombone a smooth full-bodied break
Art Horace & Pettiford bass shake & bake

on Kenny's warm dreamy "Lotus Flower"
Silver to enervate all with his piano intro
& soon its Homeric fruit makes J.J. blow
an indolent Odysseus in his funky bower

earlier on January 30th had cut three sides
Hank Cecil Horace & Art same as March
but Percy on bass with K on his cab rides
jotting "Echo of Spring" for New York's

winter skies staved hopeful quarter notes
tires spinning on ice as his melody floats
in lines read Every Good Boy Does Fine
F-A-C-E spaces sharp flat or natural sign

later in a Jersey studio Rudy laying down
"K.D.'s Motion" "La Villa" & "Venita's
Dance" his trumpet work solid but found
Lion decided to hold up session's release

even with Hank & Cecil in superior form
with Percy's bass wonderful in tune after
tune & Horace-Art underpinnings as ever
only in '87 to issue K playing up a storm

in two February '56 volumes KD on tour
with the Birdland Stars of Al Cohn tenor
Phil Woods' alto Conte Candoli trumpet
Ernie Wilkins' lucky charts of "Roulette"

& "Minorin' the Blues" from betting pen
of Manny Albam his "Two Pairs of Aces"
paying off on the KD-Conte 4-bar chases
a black & a white as if one another's twin

suits differ tonal quality a matching hand
a royal flush spade heart club or diamond
as both holding a deck-high numbered set
trumps any four face cards full or straight

spot in stanza above terms loaded as dice
a risk taken if rightly race & gender raise
resentful looks as a word rolls snake eyes
unintended sense explodes & writer pays

a chance worth taking not the crap-game
bet placed on the dozen pips of numbers
on a die up side win or lose it encumbers
unlike letters in a real or figurative name

hitting memory's jackpot with Dameron
whose sextet cut *Fontainebleau* in NYC
on March 9th '56 with Payne on the bary
again & Coker on 'bone Shadow Wilson

drums John Simmons bass Sahib on alto
Joe Alexander on tenor with Tadd piano
his sound impressions of palace gardens
lakes swans forests summon Napoleon's

L'Adieu of another March his 1814 exile
as fountains invaded dreams on Elba Isle
a hallucinating not "Delirium" of Tadd's
his frenzied joy no New Orleanian trad's

first chorus is Joe's with rollicking licks
then Gitler's "crackling" KD as he kicks
the proceedings into literally higher gear
satisfying with lyrical runs clean & clear

K's never again with Joe from Cleveland
a rejoiceful tenor but April 4th teams with
J.R. Monterose & his tick-tocking frolics
turn on a dime a river's flow roiling sand

K & tenorist on Chessmates as The Jazz
Prophets with Sam Jones bass Dick Katz
keys Arthur Edgehill drums on title tune
K's "The Prophet" J.R.'s pecking a boon

to omens seer-leader read in a minor key
portending close-knit unit's future venue
the Café Bohemia booking taped by Blue
Note same as when with Silver & Blakey

but now his wings spread as never before
& if blind to tongue-attacking of J.R. will
end so soon yet shows has begun to fulfill
his early signs as soothsayer reading soar-

ing bird in an upper region unexplored by
even the epic poets as he works its swing-
ingly happy theme with élan & not letting
up until with his cadenza he says bye-bye

each sideman strong in his way bold solo-
ing by Sam on K's "Blues Eleganté" & by
Dick comping till tenorist enters all aglow
to carry the torch passed to K holds it high

his "DX" as good as it gets as fast & fluid
he & J.R. both on a veritable changes tear
unriddling "I Got Rhythm" as if any druid
gushing blood of augury from bull or hare

chord progressions in a mysterious tongue
of brass & reed with the fingers & thumbs
hammering keys skins or strings as moon-
driven as tides percussing at night or noon

religio-pulsation seasonal as sap from root
to leaf & bud a sacred groove to all wilting
& faint of heart no Inquisition with execut-
ing of heretics or a Quijote windmill tilting

as if a benediction Billie's "Don't Explain"
lyricsless version Dick & muted K convert
to notes of a parable expresses love & pain
the hushed acceptance of happiness & hurt

session ends with K's 6/8 "Tahitian Suite"
becomes "Monaco" at the Blue Note date
of May 31 when only Katz to be replaced
by Bobby Timmons then 19 just a 2-week

rehearsal with the unit plus Kenny Burrell
on guitar not on their alternate take of this
renamed tune while K on a May 22 Signal
session with Cecil Payne doing again Diz'

"Groovin' High" better on "Saucer Eyes"
a relaxing Randy Weston theme although
at times it seems K can't get started relies
on licks from Grieg & Grofé a faulty solo

in "Bringing Up Father" "Man of Moods"
too did he miss J.R.'s tenor a minor blues
could have since with his own "Monaco"
at Café Bohemia both the horns really go

after Bob & K in an easygoing Latin beat
K changing to his intensely driving swing
a double-timing but no melodramatic feat
as Feather observes K's eighth-note string

of lines broken up by graces syncopations
but all with a mood J.R.'s tenor maintains
by hard attacks end in gentler fluent turns
lion to lambkin his lesson a listener learns

"'Round about Midnight" a Monk classic
& on it KD J.R. & Bob just as good if not
better than Thelonious himself with K hot
& high but ice-age cool as after a Jurassic

& following test of mind & soul K's own
theme titled for the place earlier dreamed
he'd visit with "Mexico City" seeds sown
as had plowed planted milked or creamed

though Ken no conquistador type foretold
in the codices as a destined ruler of fertile
fields as Montezuma'd known for a while
to come from sunrise & receive with gold

then damned Uichilobos & the other gods
forbid offerings of sacrificial virgin hearts
crosses no bloody altars so rebellion starts
the avaricious drowned as against all odds

others battle to escape on causeway drop-
ping riches in saving lives a Botello warn-
ing leave or won't survive a night of horn
& whistle calls for combat-harvested crop

& would heed their own true necromancer
when Trojans ignored Cassandra's answer
to a lying Sinon & believed too in the sign
for Narvaez defeat pig's navel on its spine

like a lady at Central Market danced alone
to Lost & Nameless Ork & Eric Hokkanen
a Finn with bass electric guitar & his violin
regretted her breasts sagged to belly button

did K read Bernal Díaz del Castillo's vivid
account or of the Aztec auspice lifted a lid
on future tribes would recognize that locus
by the snake in eagle's beak atop of cactus

spotted on Lake Texcoco's swampy island
or hear paired trumpets in a mariachi band
or Copland's dance-hall *El Salón* bare feet
in that "hot spot" lent Aaron a primal beat

perhaps absorbed it through blues osmosis
since K's "Sunrise in Mexico" title echoes
Cortés's fated coming & "City" proves its
"exotic boppish flavor" may be "grooviest

item in exciting session" Feather says with
soloists up to K's setting a precipitate pace
his impetuous break declares he's ever kith
& kin with sounds of any age & every race

a gait sustained by J.R.'s turbine of a tenor
its whirls twists & turns assertive or tender
peaceful war counts no casualties as guitar
& piano disarm till K reprises the final bar

from a newer Spain to "A Night in Tunisia"
Dizzy's take on the Sahara's North African
dunes with KD's notes as if of a dust-laden
simoon prelude to storm blown out of Asia

J.R. picking up on Rousseau negress asleep
her mandolin struck chords in Picasso et al
lion had caught her scent yet to let her keep
her desert life with tenor man playing it all

then K to announce "Autumn in New York"
his eloquence evoking Duke's lyrics mingle
new-love pain & longing for a far-off castle
the darkness blessing slums & Central Park

then his & Klook's "Royal Roost" as KD's
puissant rightful proof of his co-authorship
over a Rollins "Tenor Madness" Mobley's
"Sportin' Crowd" & then to slow their clip

on Rodgers & Hart's "My Heart Stood Still"
from no ritual knife but just one look at her
as leader states the theme of that optic thrill
& solos in even eighths as a melodic master

yet mastery can't assure survival much less
control nor even success of a storied Cortés
he forced to retreat with Tlaxcaltecan allies
barbarians providing food & water supplies

as K despite the omens auspices & auguries
disbanded a standout unit gave up unable to
wrangle sufficient work & the pathetic Blue
Note royalties not even covering Union fees

yet would not give up entirely on leadership
just withdrew as Hernán & Gen. MacArthur
but came back as shrewd determined lawyer
invaded in ships Douglas w/ a stiff upper lip

& "I Shall Return" as in his own good time
K to appear the headliner on album sleeves
meanwhile joining others to place the lime-
light on their record dates also laurel leaves

on June 15th K paired with fellow trumpeter
Donald Byrd in Phil Woods' Septet Prestige
studio gig recorded in 1956 DB a newcomer
took K's Messengers seat now he their liege

the future solo star in wide demand but here
his choruses lack continuity can get hung up
in 8- or 4-bar chases where the veteran's ear
knows whither it goes gets there with no rup-

tured rhythm repeated vapid fatuous pattern
mostly on "Pairing Off" where such unusual
figures fill his break inspire then Phil in turn
to his best showcase as too from Don's final

phrase Gene Quill takes his finest alto flight
then "Suddenly It's Spring" as two trumpets
embrace the tune with Donald to hug it tight
K in bits & pieces kisses it nearly breathless

each complementing other in hard-bop style
if their gift of gab not to say it all whose has
Satch's in a way & Bird's did too for a while
if K's a lesser it presages his increasing class

before after between free-lanced with friends
July 19 with Gee again as part of his all-stars
septet date to exhibit Matt but it still depends
on sidemen will make the most of fewer bars

bring out the best in tunes of leader originals
like namesake "Gee!" the "Kingston Lounge"
"The Boys from Brooklyn" though MG hails
from Houston bayou unlike his lively sounds

on July 27th K rejoins Messenger stablemates
for Mobley's *Second Message* Doug Watkins
Blakey & Silver all together again with Ken's
smoky tone (Ira Gitler phrase) communicates

Hank's Latinized "Message from the Border"
its then bargain boots & booze today disorder
gruesome drug wars of Montezuma's revenge
but hear in mellow trumpet & tenor no binge

of decapitation just feel their "I Should Care"
Cahn ballad with Ken pouring out a heartfelt
reading hurts to listen as he & the tenor melt
an inner berg as if emissions warming the air

an answer to "Who Cares" Gershwin's lyrics
declare love matters is unconcerned firms go
under blue chips fall a feeling K would know
had cut Ira's song with his Prophets May '56

he pianist & guitarist taking cuteness in stride
all the crew as well on Harris's "Crazeology"
if tenorist squeaks in letting rip K's dizzy ride
boggles mind with its sonic speed & accuracy

& not just into strings of notes & shows it on
Mobe's easy-going "Xlento" with K opening
at its medium tempo with his swing flows on
& on an effortless thinking is simply singing

in August K recording again "I Should Care"
now on his friend Ernie Henry's debut album
but men had long before this worked together
in a Brooklyn basement practicing in tandem

perfecting brass & reed playing as if one man
by the blending as a pair enriching each other
on the ballad the horns no catch-as-catch-can
but taking turns to lead tones into one another

as Ovid's red-hair Ocyrhoe's tale runs quickly
from Aesculapius' motherless birth to her say-
ing his curative power would soon heal sickly
till gods check her chants & end her prophesy

brings to mind blues in Ernie's "Cleo's Chant"
where he & KD tell it like it is & shall ever be
since in every age someone will forever resent
medicinal gifts or of speech or musical artistry

& something there is cuts short an Ernie's life
at 31 & even earlier Clifford Brown's only 25
who had they lived as long as the others alive
a decade later both would then have been rife

with awards have surely achieved even more
reached to higher rungs up the ladder of jazz
yet what Who's Who's to say for sure or has
had a predictive vision past the future's door

had Kenny died before he took Miles's place
with Bird or would take over Brownie's chair
with Max & encyclopedia devoted less space
to reporting his briefer career would any care

even when Roach would pick him as the one
to replace the irreplaceable heir to the throne
all bemoaned an apparent king with so much
promise barely listened to KD's Midas touch

Arriving

out of the chrysalis of bop & hard bop
K tries his wings in a '59 lower-keyed
Riverside flight with *Blue Spring* drop-
ping the temperature reducing the heat

to a balmy April day as he & Adderley
slow it down with less of Cannonball's
grandstanding sax & in his scoring KD
offers lusher lines his solo rises & falls

in "Spring Is Here" not above the staff
more often into earthier tones as tubers
root in a compost heap & as purple saf-
fron flowers from mold the cucumbers

watermelon sweet as bee pollen basket
keeps the cycle alive with KD's Septet
doing the same but minus pyrotechnics
just tendril-quick runs in his "Poetic"'s

tender strain as David Amram's French
horn warms the chords & Cecil's lyrical
baritone booms lighter with Cannonball
rushing before then letting go a drench-

ing rain of reedy notes a feeding of ears
with his kernels of gold nourish beyond
the metal itself a richer growth no pond
whose view to bream crop duster blears

by a chemical spray on one-time stream
had flowed pristine as his alto after K'd
come first with both testing the extreme
limits of instruments the two had played

& though they've gone still blowing yet
through electric outlet amplifier speaker
set-up of mid-range with bass & tweeter
each's breeze a greening fruit-giving jet

Cedar Walton's piano at times Brubeck-
ian for like their leader a versatile Texan
Adderley at his best on "Spring Cannon"
K named for him on chases neck & neck

was it at this session he heard the altoist
yodel *la-d-odle la-d-odle* as he said he'd
heard the Bird before but first farm folks
after sacks of bolls he pulled & weighed

or off the range a cowboy at end of day
back at the corral uncinching his saddle
yet unlike sax K's horn not able to play
the *ye-o-dle de* yodel of cotton & cattle

on his "Passion Spring" he & C hand-in-
glove with Ken soloing down low again
yet more exploratory a Taylor influence
could be & a Cannonball deeply intense

on "It Might as Well Be Spring" K feel-
ing Rodgers' gay-melancholy lover tune
now truly sets his indelible staccato seal
on a fever season's never come too soon

in '58 having donned his teaching gown
his class on August 29 '59 goes to town
in Berkshires' Lenox School music barn
woods & hills once home to Hawthorne

& Melville too when he wrote his epical
prose if K didn't know Herman's Whale
or of humpbacked "inveterate composer
of song" the cetacean sounds of exposer

of danger above or a call below for love
he taught them in a way to students from
Pete Farmer to trumpeter Don Cherry of
his/Ornette's *The Shape of Jazz to Come*

Ken saying of the Lenox mentor system
when he'd come to NYC had there been
such one-to-one instruction to show him
the ropes would have begged to be let in

as to the October 26 live Randy Weston
Five Spot session the less said the better
to a blue Monday add its dreary weather
its charts by a hospitalized Melba Liston

no time to run through a "High Fly" first
as Hawk & Roy Haynes' flights delayed
great tenor just warming up yet had paid
his dues could do that piece unrehearsed

together with K's horn a gorgeous sound
the two produce but in soloing over stop-
time piano chords Ken can be heard pop-
ping clams when he too had been around

for before & after KD's hooking up with
Bean another Coleman Hawkins moniker
out of a long '23 to then legendary career
the trumpeter a mainstay of saxophonists

of whatever persuasions from Swing-age
florid romantic to the Bird's cerebral bop
or the raucous soulful roar 'Trane so pop-
ularized with copycats taking up his gage

can count some three dozen reed men K
had recorded with & wonder what other
trumpeteer joined so many from Mobley
Moody Rollins Monterose Heath brother

Jim to Land McLean Dolphy Henderson
leaving out an Ernie Henry lesser known
but K paired with any gave each his best
assisted all to shine on east coast or west

had never met Oliver Nelson when studio
called Ken to come in for the October 30th
quintet date with tenor from St. Louie Mo
had "been through the big band mill" with

units like the Nat Towles & Louie Bellson
always sitting in an alto chair till switched
to his larger axe though this lower weapon
heard to cut lyrically as that higher pitched

taking the edge off the bigger's harder bite
& making it into Jack Maher's softer quite
gentler carver his "salty dog" as on Ollie's
opener his own original "Jams and Jellies"

where KD plays his "pin wheels of sound"
needing the bread but ready to lend a hand
dependable in any supporting roles as here
he sustains "Passion Flower" "atmosphere

of [Billy Strayhorn] impressionism" while
tenor mixes slow & fast with "reverential"
in this ballad's "real" Ellingtonian "voice"
& with K muted the due respectful choice

then on "Don't Stand Up" K's open bright
happy tone perfectly matching Ollie's own
a rendering of his original theme o so right
& his break few tenors have ever outshone

O's "Ostinato" a fuller showcase for a KD
solo filled with an authoritative coming on
yet is equaled & even yes outdone by Ollie
pours it on with his quoting & snappy tone

as for "What's New" could say some more
but have gone into its loveliness heretofore
so add on "Booze Blues Baby" all at home
on this funky closing tune O's as if shalom

with November 13th *Quiet Kenny*'s arrival
as on this album with just his horn accom-
panied by piano bass & drums Ken's trum-
pet now to measure up in no sense of rival-

ry with any had proven their worth before
but brings to bear on a song a predecessor
had left his stamp upon a KD new-minted
responsive mood not a reading reinvented

the case with "My Ideal" a tune the Hawk
had cut in '43 & K had heard with "Body
& Soul" from '39 the tenor's peerless talk
via fifths tonic bridge a smidge of melody

but on that later piece Ken the one's more
moving with muted tones more than stack
up with a Bean's lush rhapsodic runs lack-
ing in K's restraint his passion never over-

done but with one deep-felt poignant note
his a voluminous speech as too a selective
Flanagan piano tone or a full chord of five
fingers can touch & leave a catch in throat

on his own "Blue Friday" K low & bluesy
an open horn altered as if muted or maybe
with a hand in bell his varied sound a case-
book blues prescriptive of phase or phrase

lovely the only word for Kenny on "Alone
Together" a tune for Maher closer to home
since K recalled his doing it first with Bird
here drops so low hits a rock-bottom nerve

with "I Had the Craziest Dream" Ken join-
ing the ranks of voices exceptional even in
a music as unique as American jazz whose
tongue speaks instant sense in pop or blues

bending his notes for their delicious blend-
ing of happy & hurt now making his mark
yet not as Harry James in '42 had depend-
ed more on soaring high as morning's lark

K rather digging deeper into emotive veins
exploring the subterranean subtlety of tone
in a melodic mother lode of the tune's own
harmonic mine layered with a lover's pains

& even if must doubt those overseas troops
would've sent in '43 their constant requests
from Canal or carrier or bombardier groups
for K's rendition of that song Helen Forrest

sang with HJ's band as soldier or sailor ded-
icated the Hit Parade lyrics to a pretty nurse
or the sweetheart hoped still waiting to wed
her snapshot publicity would never disperse

as it did that Betty Grable iconic pin-up shot
of her in her bathing suit leering back so hot
with her Lloyd's insured million-dollar legs
Harry married that year of nostalgia & pegs

Kenny's therapeutic lines would just as well
have rehabilitated limbs or a wounded heart
if his light staccato soothing at a lower level
it lingers longer to lessen loss & being apart

& if not Warren-Gordon's tune K's Willard
Robison "Old Folks" version they'd ask for
again after he & Roach had played it before
in the plaintive slow swing impossibly hard

for those never achieving his effortless ease
a crackling concise unflashy & ever sincere
cantando telling of a corn-cob tale to please
& relieve to presto hope rallentandoing fear

if in his *Beggar's Opera* Gay seizes the day
sings "Beauty's a flower despised in decay"
his lyric itself as KD's album has yet to fade
as true songs survive on or off of Hit Parade

Satch's '55 "Mack the Knife" on that A side
of his first single to reach high as number 20
sold a million plus & not until "Hello Dolly"
did he hit top ten prior to the inevitable slide

Ken's of course cannot confuse with Louie's
whose vocal did the trick more than his horn
with its unmistakable its irrepressible breeze
ever blows its freshness & balm so unforlorn

letting forget for a moment a Brechtian shark
lying in wait with its pearly out-of-sight teeth
while K in modulating could dive underneath
to uncover light rays piercing a heartless dark

for as with Satch & Sonny Kenny too finding
even in such unlikely singing the silver lining
with Rollins in '56 turning a Weill's "Moritat"
from a deadly deed into his own colossal blat

on that jaunty violent song as on the Debussy
K beaten to the punch by S's whimsical tenor
& would be again in '57 on a Johnny Mercer
classic meant for Ken who outside the movie

of '36 when Bing had sung its satirical lyrics
knew *Rhythm of the Range* from real stirrups
no stunt-man routine of swingin' on a mount
& dashin' in clouds of dust right out of town

& unlike Teagarden's "I'm an Old Cowhand"
of that same year with lipped trombone turns
& melodious cords punching the witty words
K's is a sophisticated give-&-take self-call-&-

response lyrical asking-answering dialogue
with bent flutter-tongued half-valved notes
conversing both with an Andy Adams' Log
& Westminster chimes to Parliament votes

taking serious the Big Ben ring where Jack
in his vocal played up JM's amusing rimes
ranging up to date in Ford V-8 not no hack
no doggies roped got along to beef betimes

never back home whereas Newk on his sax
trail drives with cutting honks rawhide lash
a swing man skirts the herd to have it think
it's unrestrained fully free to graze or drink

on January 10th of '60 K takes over the lead
rides the point in heading the steers to cross
on solid rock not into muddy creek at a loss
of weaker stock & to turn cattle's stampede

into milling ends the run then bedding them
down on Mercer's English tune a KD brand
seared on top converted to a hard-bop hymn
an anthem to remuda quirt & the Rio Grand'

& if afterwards had recorded no other cover
just as those Goodnight Loving & Chisholm
hoofprints're bound to be followed by lover
of longhorn lore this track on *Arrival* album

to stand ever a landmark of KD's musician-
ship since it alone if no other will surely en-
dure for showing clear as wagon-wheel ruts
his inspired breath-control his blood & guts

yet album offers too K's own "Stage West"
chased at breakneck speed as if by outlaws'
gang or redskin raid & "Song of Delilah"'s
a quieter muted K with "When Sunny Gets

Blue" showcasing Charlie Davis's baritone
leader's generosity become a second nature
though wish would've done it himself alone
except for rhythm as he did with the Mercer

& does with "Lazy Afternoon" as Flanagan
opens & closes with a hazy piano just quiet
enough to hear grass growing & daisies riot
as K mutes an unembellished melody again

& "Stella by Starlight" too on his *quiet* side
& then on Manny Albam's funky "Six Bits"
another winner from a gambler true & tried
K & Charlie totally together everything fits

the same two horns hooking up in February
on 11th & 12th to record *Jazz Contemporary*
six tunes in stereo for Time "For those who
dare" plus unreleased "Sign Off" in "exclu-

sive sound extra" the label declares pianist
now Steve Kuhn & on the first three out of
six issued tunes Jimmy Garrison as bassist
but on "Horn Salute" "Tonica" "This Love

of Mine" it's again Butch Warren & drum-
mer Buddy Enlow as too the month before
Kuhn's piano K had heard as an instructor
at the Lenox August '59 for Steve an alum

who then with Ron Brown comped behind
Ornette & Cherry on "The Sphinx" & "Inn
Tune" of Margo Guryan & who heard Ken
telling his students to be inquisitive to find

& learn formation of every chord & then to
run its scale & break it up into what makes
sense to get a rhythmic feel like land sakes
alive so top to bottom all you'll play is you

true of K who'd practice what he preached
as on his tune "A Waltz" on which he mad-
ly swings from a ¾ into 4 as alkali leached
from ash for b'iled soap as the granger had

Ken's "breathtaking swoop" Mark Reilly's
phrase "ringing" with "clarity & rich emo-
tion" while Kuhn surprises with his tempo
& feeling abruptly changed so fully please

if Charlie on bary squeaks a bit he was not
K's first but his second choice since Heath
couldn't make the gig but if Davis beneath
leader's excitement level he isn't God wot

with a gruffish yet tender tone on his won-
drous rendering of the Thelonious "Mood"
"Monk's" i.e. a most moving solo for con-
templation Kuhn's touchingly pensive too

the whole group tight & showing a proper
respect to one & all but K's show-stopper
chorus an authentic individuality "simmer-
ing" Mark's word with Monkish signature

in handkerchief corner "designedly dropt"
as Walt brought to a boil by that Emerson-
ian thought & to compose his *Leaves* from
reading "The Poet" when universe stopped

but on "In Your Own Sweet Way" Charlie
can't get started with Brubeck's tune cov-
ered in '56 by Miles & 'Trane though KD
had not heard that earlier version with lov-

ing muted tones from Miles' harmon push-
ing Eros' button the tenor's sweeping licks
unlocking melodic line without romantic's
mush yet amorous in his caressive whoosh

K more playful but sticking close to theme
as Miles did for to K too melody the thing
Bru by keeping away from clichés staying
fresh & K said liked bary as other extreme

to his own high notes while Kuhn to prove
adventurous here & on KD's "Horn Salute"
with its "choppy jagged" military phraseol-
ogy Kenny knew yet better bop's "Crazeol-

ogy" a Benny Harris tune Bird had maybe
played for Pannonica in a same hotel room
where K rehearsed & from there could see
Hudson & Jersey hills as whiffed perfume

used in her mixed-media paintings of milk
acrylic & Scotch & doing them while Ken
& the men went over his "Tonica" written
for her as jazz Baroness whose Jewish gilt

had taken Monk in who phoned physician
for Bird felt his flickering beat heard thun-
der clap as Doctor came too late musician
gone yet alive on walls sound never done

though neither K ensemble nor solo lines
seem to recall his former bebopping boss
whose choruses had gotten by heart signs
missing K meant to revisit her day of loss

that weekend when she was looking after
a ragged Bird watched TV when laughter
at a juggling act on Tommy Dorsey show
broke blood loose choked & laid him low

earlier in '55 at Birdland in Ross Russell's
report Bud Powell is stewed Bird as well's
deep in his cups as Ken Blakey & Mingus
try to save the All-Stars date till KD tucks

his horn underneath an arm off to the side
of the cursing legends had befriended him
but now unable to help either one of them
ill past his cure must just move on if cried

back then or here in this nearly 3-minute
gift to her only with Butch's wistful bass
just a throb not a sorrowing sob no hint it
miffed KD when Bird gave Red his place

which leaves his CD's final piece his *sui
generis* rendition of "This Love of Mine"
with its fetching distinguished just lovely
tone his charming staccato so utterly fine

& same be said for the Harold Land date
of July 5th & 8th when as a stocking mate
perfectly matched to Houston-born tenor
San Diego-raised K & he one fitting pair

"so close" on their "So in Love" as Cole
Porter's lyrics say while Clarence Jones
on bass pushes & pulses & Ken's whole
solo's full of euphonious priceless tones

as he hits every note right on the money
undergirded on piano by an Amos Trice
a Joe Peters on drums two who not only
lend ample swing but more than suffice

with the pianist's own waltz the second
tune a piece he entitled "Triple Trouble"
& on which the horns together a fecund
duo sways in tune rich grain not stubble

on David Raksin's "Slowly" the tenorist
bringing out the theme of poignant love
then speeding it up for a blowing above
& beyond his solid work maybe his best

then Kenny still more touching yet light
in spirit as Trice turns in a splendid solo
of Clarence's bass chorus a simple ditto
with horns closing so romantically right

though "On a Little Street in Singapore"
lacking aroma of a "lotus-covered door"
held in embrace by pale perfumed hand
no temple bells in K no exotica in Land

but back to their habitat in "Okay Blues"
can hear them at home with K's pinched
tone emotes in honor of Orrin Keepnews
here not a player would ever be benched

so KD arrived & on December 9th at last
tenor Jimmy Heath pianist Kenny Drew
Garrison bass & Art Taylor drummer do
another set for Time a Kern whistle blast

of light-hearted *Show Boat* tunes with all
aboard steaming along to Jerry's musical
with Hammerstein lyrics based on Ferber
her '26 novel with sidemen K would aver

the best he had picked for any albums yet
all hanging loose but with a surging drive
& with a refreshing vibe brings love alive
in songs Jerome had to pen with no regret

can hear in any why K had wanted Heath
but most of all in "Bill" when the tenorist
nearly steals the show as he flips & twists
& soars till Ken returns to win the wreath

with shifting tacks as in trimming of sails
for running the bow into wind for sudden
directional change a self-conversing nails
high to low close-hauled notes his caden-

za a trophy-cup end to the tune & session
began with "Why Do I Love You" telling
piano comping percussion unpell-melling
& bass pulsing a steady tasty punctuation

as tenor "full-throated" a K "more supple"
to quote Nat Hentoff's insert notes groove
alone or together a complementary couple
married by & unto jazz may none reprove

on "Nobody Else But Me" KD's bending
of tones Jimmy'll answer with a blending
of matching bends each filled with a feel-
ing for love's root chords harmonies heal

on "Can't Help Lovin' That Man" a ca-
pacity for gentleness flows this an alter-
ing of Hentoff phrase with K's unfalter-
ing expressive force a lyric emotive ca-

ressive rush a Mississippi pouring forth
as Williams wrote on Hernando's corse
later Crane's "hosannahs silently below"
in nearing docks the paddlewheels slow

to "Make Believe" & a stevedore Drew
not stomping as Duke but with keys un-
loading a *Cotton Blossom* not forgotten
"dartingly humorous" ever fresh & new

as flawlessly K states still lovely theme
his nuanced shapes & shades surprising
so & as only its metal & reed can swing
Heath's tenor renews any lover's dream

then horns together on "Ol' Man River"
toting barge & lifting bale to lend relief
to past injustice yet more would deliver
for here & now their firmly held belief

no self should wish being someone else
& by riding the deepest current of Kern
to render its real & ideal tones & return
to dock & reveal them within all selves

just as Razaf's "Christopher Columbus"
sighted by the sextant in a sailor's song
so K would see he had not gone wrong
to take tune & lyrics as a truer compass

pointed to the invitation soon from afar
to voyage abroad with blue minor scale
bag packed to travel with a musical tale
chord in head & fingers his guiding star

Zodiacing

4 June of '68 nine days after the Summit
Barry Harris' Sextet with KD on trumpet
records *Bull's Eye* the Motown leader-pi-
anist's "shooting match" that's musically

speaking & Gardner's apropos liner notes
also say Kenny's first record with Barry's
friend Charles McPherson two associates
in Detroit latter altoist then but now totes

a tenor in session Don Schlitten produced
opening with Barry's title tune at extreme
up-tempo yet never too fast for a spruced-
up K who has in sight that targeted theme

lets fly first with his "superb articulation"
his speed & flow would've knocked Bird
out on remembering him from back when
he & Ken drovered together heading herd

Charles even compared with other Chazz
when he'd played on occasion a tenor too
as McPherson here & deserves such a ku-
do for his handling horn as well as he has

on baritone Pepper Adams can rarely con-
vince with his sound or sense though adds
a depth to ensemble's tone & PA has won
in Mark's liners a pat on the back ee-gads

here Barry recalls Bud Powell's phrasing
& chords in a sizzling chorus but's better
timeless could say on "Clockwise" where
it's just a trio with Higgins all're praising

& Chambers soloing arco is laudable too
while on "Off Monk" Barry with his bou-
quet paid to that prophet himself imitates
the rhythmic & tonal ways M deliberates

only a Pepper squeak to mar the homage
though made up for by K & tenor's com-
plementary play with trumpeter's engag-
ing lines relaxed but virile top to bottom

& McPherson a reminder how the Mobe
could fit with Ken hand-in-glove & now
the tenorist swinging on a similar bough
another pea in a pod or the pinna to lobe

Barry's "Barengo" is a "sinuous tango"
jazzed up by bary's anchor as KD leads
on this piece is after his heart with lingo
known from S.A. tour had planted seeds

clear from his later solo so relaxed once
more & yet all over his horn as he hunts
for & finds the Latin pulse he had heard
firsthand in New World Ken discovered

yet a land well known too to tenor man
who's conversant in its native speech as
even Pepper with his baritone more fas-
cinating with its slower "scorching" can

also be & a Harris piano with an almost
Kenton kind of "Peanut Vendor" riposte
& then a fine trio version of "Off Minor"
classic they render in Thelonious' honor

before they conclude with "O So Basal"
shows again why so many had invited K
to participate in recording sessions as all
knew could depend on him in every way

to lead or follow contribute a solo or sup-
port another's & never selfish nor fanatic
of a single style neither manic nor erratic
with talent to spare but no way puffed up

his chorus a super display of every tech-
nique in his bag of tidbits his gift for sur-
prise ever delights no notes for the heck
of it & after the "pregnant pause" juicier

with tenor bary & piano all too offering
breaks "trenchant" or "spiky and mean"
a "hip" quote before Hig drums to bring
it home the last note KD's long & clean

at the end of July on the 30th to be exact
K will appear at NYC's Top of the Gate
with pianist Toshiko Akiyoshi a live act
of those + reed bass & drums still in '68

the first piece her own "Opus No. Zero"
nothing of Japan but of a "stop-and-go"
Blakey Messengers' "hard bop rhythm"
as on it Dryden's put a finger or thumb

with Ken himself as he carries the load
stating its theme with lift strong as ever
flexing his chorus as anytime he soloed
in chase takes on Lew Tabackin's tenor

& in playing "How Insensitive" straight
with Lew on flute after the piano embel-
lishes Jobim tune they like waves swell-
ing subsiding rise fall intensify or abate

for "The First Night" K more meditative
following the piano & flute in a classical
vein & before his-Lew-drum's explosive
notes break up a spell properly nocturnal

on "Phrygian Waterfall" Toshiko to solo
with left-hand ostinato keeps modal flow
but on her "gospel-drenched" "Let's Roll
in Sake" into Nat-Cannonball kinda soul

with a demanding part for Ken but never
anything to sweat for K for certain could
cut any given if no solo here will feature
him on their next tune as well she should

since K made "Morning of the Carnival"
almost his own not Bonfá's song a piece
he'd recorded at home & abroad & as al-
ways his flutter-tongue to lend new lease

on the listener's life & with his sixteenth
notes on Tosh's "My Elegy" his strength
& total control still intact his chorus fast
as any he played to play long as he'd last

Brownie lost to accident Lee to homicide
Booker to a kidney disease awaiting Ken
& on previous April 4th the assassination
of Dr. King same decade Kennedys died

Martin's eclipse under the astrology sign
of Aries the ram whose image on *Zodiac*
Donna Jordan drew first in order to align
her sleeve-art figures with monthly track-

ing of the twelve constellations secondly
'cause 12/16/68 album begins with Cecil
Payne's in memoriam MLK on bass Wil-
bur Ware Al Heath drums Wynton Kelly

piano & with CP on both baritone & alto
as KD pays tribute with his opening solo
to the Man who had his mountain dream
in Duke song lyrics none to tear its seam

not in Nashville not anywhere even if he
like Moses kept from that promised land
for thrown in Birmingham jail made free
at last all coloreds Jim Crow had banned

at times K's burred tone & slight vibrato
seem to sob for him his notes shudder on
coming down tremble a keen high to low
at others his lines lament & yet all blown

with his jubilating flow in celebration of
a life elected though aware it would lead
to a James Earl Ray out of belief in need
for non-violence justice & Christian love

on bary Payne carries on his own mourn-
ing for that peaceful protest marcher torn
apart by that high-powered NRA's sacred
Second's right to bear Klan-armed hatred

Cecil's gruff low tones with Kelly's elec-
tric piano underscoring grief of Thoreau-
Gandhi disciples at fall of another heroic
follower yet comforted by where he'd go

far for sure from "Girl, you got a home"
& yet this second Cecil tune moving too
although in another way as he & Ken to-
gether besting K with any other baritone

their sound unmatched by either Adams-
K or Davis-K & in soloing Payne terrific
from beginning to end neither bim-bams
thank you mam nor quick flim-flam trick

& then a relaxed KD with superior swing
& more so again after a "pregnant pause"
as Kelly's chords contribute to the cause
for his unrushed blue notes keep it going

"Slide Hampton" a letdown where Ken's
concerned his brief break's not up to par
yet up to speed is Payne both his engines
firing first on bary then alto bar-after-bar

on "Follow Me" another Cecil up-tempo
his bary solo still more daring as now he
just lets go & how K takes in after him o
me o my with turns of phrases o so witty

& once Ware & Heath have traded fours
Al sets off alone to do his drummer thing
before the final piece the leader's "Flying
Fish" with pectoral fins for wings it soars

as does the whole quintet to a rumba beat
or some dance done in a Caribbean street
Cecil's bary solo lifted out of tropics' sea
& into flight by Wynton Wilbur & Tootie

while Kelly's piano chorus so plenty fine
& on ending the session K brings his feel
for the Afro-Latin rhythm with Al cosign-
ing the notes with subtly crashing cymbal

& then in spring of '69 Ken with thirteen-
year-old Donna's dad on Clifford's "new
phase" Dolphy series recording of "872"
recalls the tumultuous year's tragic scene

with another Tet attack & Black Panther
militant stand shooting of Huey Cleaver
in exile Hilliard too Seale Hoover F.B.I.
& near the end Hampton & Clark to die

but Ken just part of ensemble sound not
taking an in-yo'-face nor any angry solo
never one to complain wonder still what
he thought of radicals racist pigs & Mao

did he side in his mind more with a King
or with Carmichael's Black empowering
or reject imperiling his teeth as Satchmo
said he'd do no good if he couldn't blow

on his tenor Jordan now up to date on all
the enraged & raw-toned raucous school
ousts bop & fist-pumps death to the cool
but hear in his notes less hate than usual

& on Cliff's "Quagoudougou" the lower
tones on his horn his trill a sudden honk
& picked-off high-up pitch deliver more
of a point than any urge to bonk or conk

then K to work out his own "new phase"
yet after two kinds of bop no other craze
came natural to him though still to show
he could do it too & was willing to grow

his solo even so doesn't swing not up to
his older routine & Julian Priester trom-
bone break nothing great while Wynton
with his groovy rock fits into old or new

two drummers Ed & Roy rambunctious
while the tenor's best here *In the World*
whose trend then Ken resided in for just
this once before eviction notice unfurled

with his final performance in August '70
his chops Yanow writes were failing him
on playing at Roosevelt College in mem-
ory of a Bird's 50th birthday anniversary

& never again would K record his sound
one never made on earth by any trumpet
even if better players to come had found
his horn or its brand none would make it

& even though he pauses more the spark
still there & on "Summertime" will hark
back to the old fire of those earlier years
with legends Yard 'Trane & all his peers

but first "Just Friends" with his scintillat-
ing runs & that burnished tone can never
mistake for another's can never overrate
its warmth or his ever getting it together

& then Ken introduces in his tenor voice
to be taped no more for the listener alive
the Gershwin as Ray Nance's violin jive
opens its bluesiness for which all rejoice

if KD's stamina's beginning to fade still
to hear him every trumpeteer must envy
the sustained power of an unbowed will
in honoring a mentor with such melody

remembering through every trill & tone
a note shaken up high held long or short
all the Bird solos he had gotten by heart
before arriving in NYC a near unknown

his mark made when his star would rise
if not in a CP sky jazz gazers so idolize
& if not to inspire scrawls of "KD lives"
yet his a musical gift still gives & gives

Expiring

all the breaths once taken in & then let
out for words sung notes from trumpet
those tongued staccato or emitted long
for a sharp flat accidental natural song

the airflow divided up in bars of duple
triple quadruple time the tones to vary
in length & mood observing as a pupil
signatures for meter & to read the key

a life's continuum early middle & late
though still four years from fifty when
had to take work as a music-store ven-
dor & postal clerk with no record date

his cabaret card had lost & on dialysis
union dues unpaid membership expir-
ing meant no blood transfusion all this
while the girls grew up then NYU hir-

ing him as part-timer brought in some
& liked teaching but its pay minimum
had been to Austin for their Longhorn
Jazz Festival April 28-30 '67 perform-

ing with the Sam Houston State Band
had written for June *Down Beat* issue
his report on that event its who's who
from Monk Diz & Blakey to outstand-

ing fellow Texans Arnett Cobb Clean-
head Vinson Jimmy Ford Buddy Tate
Cedric Haywood & Charles Patterson
Teddy Wilson native hometown great

Ernie & Emilio Cáceres Larry Coryell
the Bayou City-raised Illinois Jacquet
plus drum legend Jo & the modern El-
vin unkin Joneses together for one set

of Jo wrote had played "with the ease
and grace that kings are made of" Art
"fuerte y con mucho fuego" & on part
of the young "White Power" 21-piece

"supporting cast" said for it & K boss
arrangements that audience screamed
his "what else?" shows never at a loss
for drollery as language too esteemed

even hoped to write or to play his way
to Diz's tremendous level & for '70 K
to produce indeed his so fine too-brief
modest memoir fragment's self-belief

the next year or the one after to phone
Austin's University to say might relo-
cate he'd enjoy playing in its jazz pro-
gram & helping band students to hone

their skills had plans for setting up his
treatments here D. Goodwin directing
the ensemble then & remembered this
having arranged prior to KD's passing

his "Epitaph" & performing that chart
at Chicago's national college jazz fes-
tival in '72 K December 5th breathless
from renal failure had stopped a heart

a brain filled with unseen notes heard
within his inner ears then out of tubes
through his silver bell his valve lubes
had speeded along Messengers' word

a prophetic phrase blues or bossa beat
a chase or a smoky-toned running line
to blend with any instrument compete
with none but under the brothers' sign

Cecil Payne recalling at K's Brooklyn
family-man home he taught him a roll
& toodle on baritone looked sick skin
color *very* dry last seen at jazz mobile

studio where all there but Kenny grip-
ing about a musician's economic state
he *quiet* just holding his horn no hype
with him had accepted his chosen fate

had taken him from Post Oak to NYC
then 'Frisco Paree Scandinavia Brazil
to the lyrics learned & by them to feel
to the recorded sounds he will ever be

from *María's Book*

María's Albums

narrate the stories of two lives together
of children half-Texan she came to bear
from a fated union of our cultures differ
her own in Chile she left behind forever

on their pages each's disparate thought
mine in the accent of a Scottish brogue
a softer & warmer her Spanish brought
combined in binders covered with cloth

patterned prints on spines embroidered
with dates all begin & end each January
each tracing months from the same 28th
& its celebration of another anniversary

with flowers bought & books inscribed
the suppers eaten out & movies at times
in a B & B smokehouse spending a night
a gift of the kids saved quarters & dimes

memories recorded from places had lived
mostly towns & cities she'd never choose
only treasured for where a first word said
quiet or trying moments not about to lose

so determined all those she must preserve
yet complains there isn't the time it takes
for selecting the photo will better capture
the son & the daughter at each special age

the leisure needed for her writing by hand
drawing her pictures to replace those miss
stolen when the family had moved by train
a worthless box of snapshots o so priceless

the death of pet or relation the greater loss
recounting each with a photograph recalls
a dog cat or the needles would dip & cross
as Gala knitted before a final evening walk

phrases jotted down from elementary tales
Ms. Foy's "I'm sick & tired" said to a class
how fit them in between the fixing of meals
doing laundry & the endless dishes to wash

with ironing awaiting after her library work
no hours left for assembling of each souvenir
of her teenage violinist in Mozart's Salzburg
her ballerina danced in an annual *Nutcracker*

her job part-time but her cooking never ends
weeding & watering of beds in need of a rain
others to make & all that mopping & dusting
darning of sox a tub & sinks scrubbing clean

yet her colorful volumes all but filling a case
scrapbooks spanning decades now nearly four
notes in an unadorned prose of a natural grace
composed in her tongue some have rated poor

though rich to any readers of her native words
those all blessed by her annals & a selflessness
in collecting sedulously both sad & humorous
crammed into the space her only closet affords

María's Dresses

no matter their prices or how they've looked
found hanging on dismal bargain-store racks
stacked for sale in a stranger's garage or yard
in the end all alike have been transformed

not alone by laundering & changing a hem
by adding a bow or redoing a gaudy collar
by letting the waist out or by taking it in
but by covering clinging & softly conforming

like the simple white of that wedding day
made from her own design by her Tía Pepa
only showed her bare tanned arms between
her short sleeves & gloves of cotton netting

silk organdy to the throat & down to the floor
trimmed with the velvet sash of peaches pink
laced ruffle over tips of delicate slippered feet
a ribbon held her hair & the eagerly lifted veil

María's Genealogy

a lapsed Catholic herself
somewhat like her mother
who never went to mass
but ever offered a prayer

yet if unanswered right away
quickly appealed to another saint
though at least her younger daughter
has attended on the two big dates

his winter birth & springtime death
though instead of the Roman church
has kidded perhaps she may convert
to the polygamous Latter-Day faith

smiles to remember in Chile
how all along her Pyramid Street
neighbors would yell in warning
then close their shutters & doors

at the coming of an identical
white-shirted necktied pair
though always one short one tall
appearing each year to explain

in broken Spanish the origins of
their sacred *Book of Mormon*
though saddened now to recall
a young man murdered in Austin

who had served his time by walking
each unfriendly belligerent block
to bring the news to every race
others sent farther for photographs

of the records of married & deceased
in every out of the way diocese
Ovalle where on January 12th of '44
Gala was delivered of my pride & joy

her second girl child who prefers
dusty La Chimba to anywhere else
another unheard-of country place
her grandfather's in the little north

needed to know of its former life
ways her mother had had to go
which train she took to school
in the southern town of Rengo

wanted as well to identify
those her line descended from
& to find them had to drive
to their Family History Center

to order from Salt Lake City
handwritten archives on microfilm
to view in Texas the Chilean names
to decipher five centuries of entries

for reconstructing her Aguirre tree
all the wedded cousins & their issue
the generations on her maternal side
down to her own & her sister's too

tracing back to 1540 when out of Perú
Francisco most loyal captain to Valdivia
crossed with that conqueror the Atacama
second worst desert in all the world

born 1500 in Talavera de la Reina
he her first relation in Chile
governor-defender of La Serena
defeated Drake & his buccaneers

had marauded her native coast
burning homes & inventories
accurately kept for every parish
her forebears born & buried

Paco later mayor of Santiago
capital city where she came to accept
for this gave up her storied nation
here where she's read how at sixty-nine

he lay imprisoned in La Plata
awaiting three years for delayed release
by order of the King would hear & respond
to news they had dragged his faithful servant

before the Inquisition in Chuquisaca
marched in chains from Tucumán
back across the Andes & the Atacama
to be accused of heresy in word & deed

ninety crimes against religion
among them how not hearing mass
could bring no harm to those he believed
commend in hearts their souls to God

how Plato could equal in thought
the Gospel according to the Evangel John
how excommunication frightened little men
not him who never feared dishonest priests

would eat not fish but meat on Fridays
on holidays had his Indians work the fields
declared heaven & earth could pass away
but not the truth he was pledged to say

then bareheaded forced to confess his errors
by bishop & viceroy had grown to covet
the authority vested in him by Philip II
those at last had convinced the throne

the Americas needed to sit a Tribunal
whose accusations continued till '76
when he returned to his fruits & flowers
orchards & gardens won in Araucanian wars

at 81 after 40 years & just before the end
writing from New Spain his final lines
declared he had faithfully served his sovereign
along with chattel household & offspring

spending 300 thousand of his personal pesos
losing brother sons son-in-law & grandsons
in discovering subduing & settling a kingdom
in the name of his highness whose hands & feet

his vassal kissed from the blue Pacific
of her long thin land she now revisits
by virtue of that conquistador's words
& those who trust in the power of prayer

to save them from eternal death
& every ancestor who ever lived
before that sacred revelation
of their founder Joseph Smith

María's Heart

(or whichever organ it is
hurts from what we miss)
bears the tiniest tear
in the shape of where
she was born to be
in her long thin native Chile
given up against her will
once love had made her feel
through affection's forceful sway
she had to forsake it & come away
to this foreign place as any African slave
or more like the poor & oppressed still brave
immigrant hardship as did the Irish & Russian Jews
for those of their own volition could choose
to take the risk & make the voyage
in a cramped unhealthy steerage
if surviving to land on Ellis Island
arriving barely to understand
the official exam would undergo
if answered wrong stamped mentally slow
deported alone separated from parents whose family name
anglicized by authorities & on Galveston Isle the same
quarantined & lined up all in the nude
for delousing by inspectors whose forebears earlier sued
to enter the Redman's space any indignity ready to endure
since each & every self so wonderfully sure
in its innocent soul (or whatever it is
suffers pain for future bliss)
it would soon find freedom's hope fulfilled
but with her longing for home unstilled
the rip from that rift now throbs again
its wound still seeping deep within
& all because her coming here
cut her off from a relationship first & forever dear
her maiden name replaced by mine
a Scottish on paperwork she has had to sign
on her alien card rude agents review with every trip
since she'll not surrender her Chilean citizenship
& how does it make me feel
her having come against her will
o torn in two though in the end

know she's stayed & as yet no law has passed to send
her back & so have tried to believe it's right
in the Logic-versus-Emotion title fight
the decision should go to the breakable heart
(if that's the body's irrational loving part)

María's Hem

before my barefoot contessa
will baste by hand & sew
she has me measure all around

from bottom of skirt to table top
where her seductive feet
now slowly turn

to this pinning marks
the proper length
as I kneel before this table

like the pedestal I have ever
placed her on
though to her it's just

pure sacrilege
can hear her say
they're made of clay

& yet love needles
until once more
impiety sings

her inch by
inch another
fitting hymn

María's Ideas

at first accepted few or none
almost all rejected out of hand
& automatic would prefer my own

argued hers were too much trouble
would require money we didn't have
though really just my giving in

for always it was utterly clear
hers better & made more sense
like the faithful used VW van

she conceived we ought to buy
for its side door easily slides
two seats for kids & pets

with one removed for hauling sand
gravel & her organic garden soil
to transport the tiles to replace

the dusty dirty carpets she felt
so harmful to all our health
& having learned the hard way

marriage math means a little expense
can make for a contented wife
I had paid the asking price

& then one day she thought
we needed a bit more space
yet liked no house she saw

so decided to add to this
& had me call for estimates
to expand out behind the back

the first seemed way too high
so had me phone another place
Erik arriving to hear her plan

for an addition above the garage
& leaning against his pickup truck
he quickly sketched a simple design

a room for each of us
a half bath convenient to both
hers for tables & sewing machine

mine for shelves CDs & books
into hers would move a bed
on visits from family & friends

& although Erik's bid the same
his job finished right on time
& still we're taking pleasure in

this plot too saccharine for some
one true as a tragic play's
but hers with genial comic outcome

María's Larkspur

a variety called
Cloudy Skies who
knows why when

its bloom's no
fluffy cumulus but
a spurred calyx

of pink violet
blue or white
prefers rich well-drained

soil ample water
will not the
catalog ads declare

rain on your
day but does
dislike to be

transplanted & looks
best in patches
clustered together although

unseen now in
the backyard where
she set them

out & yet
from there a
gully-washer swept their

seeds away &
ending up in
front between sidewalk

& curb they
rooted in dirt
under pea-sized gravel

her *Delphinium consolida*
a genus complex
as orchids although

absent any genetic
barrier to intercrossing
& in hybridizing

brings such comfort
as when this
month after the

deep winter freeze
had done in
her white dewdrop

duranta whose blossoms
draw butterfly bee
& hummingbird these

lifted their sepals
stamens styles anthers
pedicels & pistils

& for decades
the description says
will yield a

steady petal supply
& not for
her eyes alone

since just last
week two young
girls white &

black knelt on
this asphalt street
the latter snapping

a photograph for
lack perhaps of
beauty at home

carried their picture
to share it
with those may

have needed the
sight even more
if only as

a Kodacolor &
though the real
thing brown &

wither will yet
return with spring
& while too

my flower who
sowed them first
must fade as

any blossom her
stigmas left behind
will on another

day in receiving
pollen germinate her
bright consoling clouds

María's Maine Coon Cat

after his whiskered face
tufted cheeks striped legs
& perfectly rounded paws

appeared sitting upon
her backyard cedar bench
his huge yellow eyes

staring in hope & fear
she yearned to know
the life he lived before

then invented for him
an abusive history
of being left outside

in thunder & lightning
can lower him still
just as the sight of a

broom or stranger
will flatten his fluffy tail
make him growl &

run for cover under
dresser couch or bed
had arrived unsexed & bedraggled

& against every objection
her Siamese had been
trouble enough

she coaxed him in
to her home & heart
both taken over by

his long sharp claws
ruined the new front door
& though her skin unmarked

will kill her instead
with golden belly spread
protected along the windowsill

by crape myrtle photinia
abelia & bridal wreath
& thrills her when

the primal beast shows through
as he stalks among her
rosemary Mexican oregano

salvia & mint leave his mottled
coat matted & scented with
spent blooms her brushing removes

as she pets & kisses
& whispers in his ear
he's her sweetie pie

the most beautiful creature
in the whole wide world
who made it miraculously

from New England here
her unlooked-for gift
has brought such treasure

as no lottery she says
no fame or glory
could ever give

& it goes as well for her
who accepted my awkward
invitation to that date

will never forget
since as lucky as he
with his hope & fear

I too with mine
was not turned down
but let in to all of this

María's Movies

are none she's made herself
only those she has seen
again & again her all-time

favorite *Master & Commander* with
Russell Crowe even though she's
so opposed to violence in

life & film but can
allow it on the screen
if acting writing & cinematography

all come together as when
from his crew's cello-playing naturalist-physician
that Aussie actor learns of

an insect camouflaged as stick
or twig & disguises their
outmanned vessel as a blubber-smoking

whaler takes by complete surprise
the superior Napoleonic warship &
high too on her list

actor-director Warren Beatty as Jack
Reed in *Reds* with Diane
Keaton as Louise Bryant asks

as what would she go
with him to NYC his
wife or concubine his reply

with Thanksgiving near why not
come as a turkey Jack
Nicholson as the cynical playwright

Gene O'Neill & Henry Miller
historical witness to Communist dreams
observing with one eye closed

as much fucking went on
then as now but today
it's perverse while those showed

a bit of heart &
even love & she also
gets a kick out of

John Cusack in *High Fidelity*
with its top-ten pop-song themes
Jack Black as the record-store

clerk dresses a customer down
for his collection doesn't include
Bob Dylan's *Blonde on Blonde*

& of course Marisa Tomei
as an out-of-work hairdresser whose
biological clock's ticking away while

Joe Pesci her lawyer-fiancé knows
no courtroom procedure together in
My Cousin Vinny whose witty

script with its details like
mud in tires & cooking
grits seem only meant for

laughs but return as significant
facts & win the case
for two students wrongly accused

yet mostly she prefers to
the Hollywood epic or comic
routine such foreign-made features as

The Syrian Bride who's stopped
at the border crossing &
kept from joining her unknown

groom by the Israelis &
her own Islamic guards &
were she to leave would

not be permitted ever again
to return to her country
& this my Chilean understands

from having given up her
native land for this marriage
could have gone wrong being

resented by her countrymen from
marrying a gringo & agreeing
to go abroad with him

& suspicious here from never
becoming a citizen but ever
remaining year-after-year a registered alien

& in *The Weeping Camel*
identifies deeply with its ceremony
performed in the Mongolian Gobi

for the mother after her
difficult birth will not feed
her own white colt until

with two-stringed horse-head fiddle the
musician sings *hoos hoos hoos*
pleading with notes & words

for her to accept her
hungry offspring cries each morning
to suckle her nourishing milk

& adores *The Vertical Ray
of the Sun* with its
three Vietnamese daughters prepare their

parents' memorial banquet while each
in her way unhappy &
yet all beautifully affectively shot

one with a husband with
writer's block another whose spouse
visits his lover in his

other house the unwed youngest
living with her brother &
fantasizing she carries a child

or those like the Israeli
Lemon Tree pictures the injustice
of their Supreme Court ruling

against the Palestinian's grove on
upholding its being bulldozed down
& *Bliss* the gripping Turkish

flick of the innocent girl
secretly raped by the village
leader demands an honor killing

sends his son to pull
the trigger or force her
into a suicide leap but

fallen in love with her
he comes to hide her
till the truth will out

& the lives in *Cave
of the Yellow Dog* &
The Scent of Green Papaya

most of all in *Once*
with its music & love
sung & playacted from life

by Glen Hansard the Irish
singer & Markéta Irglová his
gorgeous Czech immigrant friend these

half-fictions real to her not
TV reality shows but more
like documentaries on rented DVDs

María's New Mexico

ever begins at the end
of the Santa Fe Trail
where trappers settlers & traders

after their thousand-mile overland trek
cheered & tossed their bonnets
beaver caps & broad-brimmed hats

high in the autumn air
on looking down at last
from the Sangre de Cristo's

snow-mantled peaks & glimpsing sight
of cottonwoods & aspens below
with leaves richer than even

Cíbola's gold their yellows Gustave
Baumann later engraved & other
artists minted in modernist oils

the Plaza where native craftsmen
display their rings & necklaces
silver & turquoise with squash-blossom

& bear-claw tabs mosaic inlay
pendants spread out on cloths
along the Governor's Palace walls

across from the sidewalk plaques
honor Georgia O'Keeffe Eliseo Rodríguez
Willa Cather Oliver La Farge

yet unlike the weary &
relieved she stops here only
briefly before she continues north

on the high road to
Chimayó Truchas Trampas & Peñasco
but Taos most of all

by that scenic route with
its poverty & collapsing homes
next to pricey galleries' art

or will take the Rio
Grande drive to Embudo &
Velarde by apple orchards at

Dixon past Stanley Crawford's garlic
farm with roadside stands offer
red chile ristras & in

spring rafters running rapids although
she never comes for sports
just heads for Mabel's home

& Couse's too to walk
again the former's grounds to
observe their surrounding trees &

the dovecote pigeons circle around
on gray-white wings to take
in against the clear blue

sky the sacred mountain Mabel
viewed from her upstairs room
for years has wished to

see inside where Brett &
the prudish Lorenzo painted the
bathroom window or on oppressive

summer days where Mabel drank
her lemonade the cozy winter
fireplace where she awaited return

of her wise & regal
Tony & comes to watch
the acequia ripple beneath a

footbridge near the hand-carved gate
saved from the Ranchos church
after the French archbishop unhinged

& removed its rustic doors
replaced them in the town's
now most illustrious tourist attraction

its sight etched painted &
photographed so many times from
not the front but the

bare backside's curved adobe slope
& must explore every nook
& cranny in the studio

where Couse would work upon
his fireside scenes with his
models either of Pueblo brothers

as if his own his
homage paid to their dignified
race & she's enamored too

of hand-cut beams & of
stone-filtered water she savors still
from Chilean summers recovered here

in this Indian-Hispanic-Anglo state with
its past to which she
feels akin since its Chama

& chamisa return her to
her youthful days in La
Chimba's dry & fruitful land

whose longed-for time & place
she visits again if only
through a museum exhibit case

María's Paint

after the novel by W.D. Howells

its label claims one easy coat's enough
to do the job as deodorant & patriotism
she calls the great American cover-ups
hide sweaty odor & a multitude of sins

but first she insists I will have to clean
with bleach & remove the grime before
I apply the light & darker green
picked from samples the hardware store

gave her free of charge she like Lapham's
wife determined to have the colors
changed on all the outside walls & trim
tired of seeing on windows & doors

the same ugly grayish brown so common
here in Texas where that protagonist came
then returned to rise & fall in his own
Vermont where Pert whose dearest name

he gave to his line of fancy shades
goaded Silas until he set a date & got
it done while week-after-week I've just delayed
the inevitable by resisting in cold or hot

as the brand she bought or the one
he sold from a rotten-tree mine his father
had lucked upon as I still put off the bother
of masking tape of loading the caulking gun

of climbing a ladder unreaches to gable tops
with enamel dropping in dribs & drips
on bifocals shirt pants sandals & sox
& of washing rollers brushes & stirring sticks

even as she assures me once I finish
I'll feel so virtuous & will love the fresher
look & this is true though any real pleasure
will only come from giving her her wish

María's Redecoration

comes twice a year
when with spring &
fall she changes to

seasonal shades as do
skies grass & leaves
repaints the shelves &

replaces light-green plates or
blue-on-white with the yellow
autumnal set & then

rearranges furniture in the
living room & washes
starches irons & fits

homemade covers on garage-sale
finds her sofa couch
& cheap love seat

takes down & alternates
framed prints & exhibit
posters with mostly Santa

Fe & Taos themes
her impressionist Connecticut scenes
or her favorite Matisse

of a young woman
seated reading a book
on a tripod table

substitutes a displayed copy
of Thoreau's *Maine Woods'*
river trips for his

Wild Fruits moving antique
crocks from above the
pantry to cabinet tops

bringing back sailboats dry-docked
in closet or garage
to launch them on

the mantel again its
fireplace rarely used in
this Texas weather removed

when her keen nose
detected the reek of
rat droppings in nests

of its pink fluffy
insulation for must have
every six months a

different look to keep
mind & eyesight fresh
while I a creature

of habit complain but
then on giving in
lift cart & resort

to the brutish force
she's ever against although
she will allow it

as a necessary helpful
ill & in the
end I must admit

such exertion does renew
the spirit but mostly
the getting to see

her creative touch with
the old décor is
all it takes to

learn change is better
than same except for
this year-round loving her

María's Smile

has remained unchanged with
age the lovely curves
of her winsome lips
two front teeth first

glimpsed in Santiago's Institute
at its check-out desk
as she stamped due
dates filled patron requests

happy in her work
searching file & record
ever ready to serve
but ID card required

can recognize it anywhere
in profile years before
standing on rubble near
mining at El Salvador

her shoed left foot
tiptoed her alluring face
with its ingenuous look
turned from desert waste

to the camera lens
a scarf covering hair
tied beneath her chin
homemade skirt & sweater

at sixteen captured in
copper country by Saul
a sweetheart from then
grateful to that rival

for his earlier lust
inscribed on this picture
his "She at Dusk"
"Ella en un Atardecer"

after our wedding giving
birth & writing kin
desperately missed on living
in places always alien

on a teacher's pathetic
pay then returned together
to visit Arica's Pacific
coast with behind her

banana leaves & waves
she in yellow sweatshirt
with red corn-kernels necklace
so beautiful it hurt

her hairline straight between
dark strands combed apart
pulled back by ribbon
& rubber band start

these thoughts of how
her mature dignified style
she insists on now
has replaced that idyll

refuses to play her
younger self to dress
as if a teenager
then gaze at this

of a second grandchild
held in her arms
here too her smile
is just as warm

tender open if anything
still brighter no gray
untinted hair no wrinkling
taking its radiance away

María's Voices

a dozen at least have come to life
on her lips I've stopped with kisses
though never meant to hold them back

each of a stuffed or porcelain doll
or of the part Pekinese & border collie
her first pet who looked like a frog

so named him Sapo her Spanish for toad
later had more of a monkey's face
with his hair behind like bloomers

flared & swayed when he wagged his tail
dead from the side gate left unlatched
his ribcage crushed by a neighbor's cur

yet still he speaks around this house
in her high-pitched doggie voice
though fully grown at ten years old

when we dug his backyard grave
under the shade of a broad-leaved tree
where he played among the honeysuckle

till now her opening & closing of lips
is a sweetening of death let out too soon
his punctured lung nearly good as new

* * *

only her Chilean family & friends
knew at the exchange of vows & rings
I had married a mother of bickering brats

never conceived how so many more
would appear besides our son & daughter
how fights between the two of them

could hardly hope to match
the insults yelled & the tantrums pitched
by cats & bears & dolls of fabric scraps

so proud of her on arriving home
just dying to show her off
to kinsfolk only knew Fort Worth

when all she cared to ask about
was where to buy a Winnie-the-Pooh
those so certain I had gotten a child

who swore I hadn't a lick of sense
needed a woman could straighten me out
not be strapped with some foreign gal

had yet to outgrow playing house

* * *

in another language they're not the same
lost is the joy of her open vowels
of the eñes trills & double ells

this Texas mutter like mush in the mouth
the way she mimics how I mispronounce
even the name of my native state

the one sure place I feel at ease
in courting days she thought it referred
to the percent of income a citizen pays

then came to where no junta caused her to
unlike those chose to take refuge
in a hated land they still berate

where her babes would inherit my brazen tongue
that is Darío & Elisa certainly not Pooh
ever brags he is British anyhoo

& reminds how the Scots eat oats
while in England where he is from
they throw them out to cow & hog

his way of driving home another point
how he is of a higher race
of the same lineage as the Avon bard

when who pipes up but Paula Alessandri Rodríguez
ex-President's daughter or so she claims to be
descended from the Republic's "Lion of Chapa Chapa Chapa"

baby talk for Arturo Alessandri Palma
how spoiled can hear from her tone of voice
she & Pooh antagonists from the very start

"You were born in a department store
at the one near T.C.U."
"Shut up fatty who asked you?

gypsies left you on the backdoor stoop"
& back & forth they go in nasty kind
till Paula begs that I take her side

then says to Pooh "They paid too much for you
all your stuffing's falling out"
reminds how he was bought where I fitted shoes

at the Cox's over on Berry Street
sent later to the one at Lancaster & Ayers
to manage the floor two blocks from where

at that rented one-bedroom
the barbecue smell kept seeping through
cooked daily across at that corner stand

a food she still can't stomach
as the reek of its hickory smoke
brings back her morning sickness

is a memory she won't forgive
& of the horned frog sat out front all day
kept her from fetching letters from home

& the tarantula ambled down the walk
when we'd go to let her stretch her legs
all those she still recalls

& won't let it be forgotten
how her cloth world with its button eyes
of Paula & Winnie-the-Pooh

has never borne such frightfulness
nor will ever contain the pain
of a pregnancy endured in Cowtown

though never once has she regretted since
the mix of her Castilian with this hick accent
in a son's harmonious coming

alive red-haired & kicking

* * *

besides Paula's rows with Pooh
who any chance he gets
will crack at her expense

jokes on how obese she is
pokes fun at her fractured face
poor thing suffers even worse

at the young dialectical hands
of Juanito the Communist boy
whose suave announcer's voice

will report on & by the hour
his same predictable party line
"I say that on that glorious day

when the Revolution takes control
the first to go will surely be
parasites like you & your Alessandri

with your only worry night & day
if your hairdo's straight
or your make-up's on

waiting to have a nursemaid serve
your midday brunch in bed
but soon enough our time will come

& then the lot of you
Granny Gala & María too
will work & eat & dress the way

the People do"

in Chile after the mere mention of Granny
his speech would abruptly end
for Rita then would interrupt

grow livid as if he really lived
whose politics she wouldn't hear
yet loved him more than all the rest

had made his fine brown two-piece suit
the one he wore each time they fought
at breakfast & dinner or at four for tea

at any meal her only care
to pick at him then hide away
the desserts she'd never eat

but kept them in her room
They're mine she'd say Why not?
rolled her own & smoked them down

till the day she died at ninety-two
argued on between her puffs
disgusted by that socialist spiel

when Juanito in his juvenile pitch
would attack with his prodigy's wit
all declared his logic best

but knew of course was just María's
all thought her destined for the bar
would write such briefs

as could not be beat
predicted how she would rise
to the country's highest bench

yet believed not a word she had him say
sister mother & every relative laughed
but marked their ballots all far right

banged their empty pans in the women's march
to oust Allende's Marxist plan
& had Granny learned that man elected

though gone before that storied date
her dinner sweets green with mold
she would have died all over again

yet still can hear her scolding him
when he delivers his leftist speech
here in this capitalist kitchen

her cigarette licked & lighted up
her custard fresh with every phrase
saved even now from & for another day

* * *

many there are have never known
the one within only she can hear
those too of dolls have not survived

from childhood towns to north & south
from Ovalle where water is sacred scarce
& Temuco where dampness stays & stays

where Gala got the habit she never broke
of holding her napkin before the stove
even when they moved where rain & snow

fall mainly in the Andes rarely down below
in Santiago where we'd meet & wed
source of her many voices in dialogue

some lost forever others picked up here
where I'd take as true Paula's invented chatter
her transposed letters of naughty words

those no Spanish-speakers ever understood
outside this home such listeners all confused
& to parrot her language made me a fool

the kids as well misled by false phonetics
by much of Pooh's grammar so incorrect
& yet a teacher's role their Mom rejects

till now we none can quite be sure
if the diction of half we've heard
is of baby puppy or chicky talk

or a child's proletariat squawk
our tongues all twisted out of shape
by imitating phrases her own creates

but need them all
& cackle on catching another mistake
the fun she makes of "O how great

how smart you think you are"

* * *

the one would hear above the rest
is day-in day-out just her own
that's the one for every season
right for every rhyme & reason

the one can make me shudder most
more than any shout or scream
in a blood-curdling horror film
is hers withheld exiled divorced

when in a pique I've sent it away
down to her dollies in Ovalle
to damp & mildew in Temuco
to that cozy home in Santiago

forensics silenced deep within
instruments capped with telling mutes
won't share or let them soothe
until I come back to my senses

but how prefer any among them all
when each is a part of who she is
as in these years she's been to the kids
playmate & mother rolled in one

to me my star of stage & screen
my keeper critic lover friend

María's Yards

her thumb is not so green as she would like
though wherever she is things grow & thrive
trees she planted still leaf out some bear fruit
the blue spruce in Hobbs an apple in Malta
& yet from a year at Voorhees one at UDLA
little more than anguish has for her survived

in New Mexico on Yeso the ground bone-dry
sandstorms blowing the topsoil off & away
on the landlady's trellis would trim the roses
while awaiting the pangs of ineffectual labor
then induced to deliver the 7-lb. 10-oz. son
later tended petunias as the hearing went on
to determine if the father would be suspended
but mostly she would let that earth lie fallow
too afraid of setting foot on the red-ant bed
with its eyes of a horned frog squirted blood

in Illinois on Orput a captive to ice & snow
November to April or on warm rainy days
stuck inside from a sidewalk rippled to life
as a mass of worms would slither & squirm
but there the daughter came gentler in birth
& there her seedlings would produce new shoots
tomatoes for *gazpacho* & okra's long furry spears
strange to farmer friends stopped by to admire
amazed by her cucumbers watermelon-sweet
deep green three months then brown & sere
lined early with frost soon coated & covered
buried beneath a white & windswept sheet

in South Carolina the apartment yard so small
her patch out back barely enough for the dog
he tied to one board of a shared wooden fence
each time she went there & set out his dish
he attacked by the unleashed bully next-door
there the poor sandy soil lay barren in shade
any sunlight blocked out by a thicket of pine
a mat of reddish needles overlaid the ground
till it choked all growth except for the weeds
while over those woods hung a humid reek
with Spanish moss strung from rotting limbs
would spook her back in to water the pots
to wash & mist the schefflera's glossy leaves

against spider mites spun their lethal webs
as administrators embezzled minority funds
one murdered some indicted one served time
she trying to keep that hole healthy & green
closing the blinds on glares from faculty cars
parked at front doors with rusting screens
maintaining her home as a refuge within
for kids pet & spouse whose only job offer
had lured her into Voorhee's alligator swamp
with peanuts & collards the only crops

then a phone call from Mexico enabled escape
to a climate & language more nearly her own
where the open-air market welcomed her way
of haggling in the smoke of fried *chicharrón*
there finding words different for familiar fare
elote for corn whose name in her Chilean *choclo*
ejote for beans she knew rather as *porotos verdes*
got a big chicken when she asked for *repollo*
instead of a cabbage for the Mexican is *col*
women with braided hair & stubby bare feet
babes on backs wrapped in handmade shawls
piled their fruit & vegetables in neat pyramids
& all clamored to have her sample their wares
a woven sack in each hand weighing her down
would carry home on foot as much as she could
past a real pyramid New World's largest known
on the trail of tears from Tula & the fish manure
from the Tree of Birth to the Stone-man's fall
diaspora from mounds of myth-sized maize
to the site of four mountains crowned with snow
where the Conquistador spilled the natives' blood
& near it in the backyard of that faculty house
borrowed while a professor on leave in Oaxaca
she'd set out Swiss chard for adding to meals
the iron in its colorful leaf & succulent stalk
but first soaked in water with iodine drops
to protect weak systems from a strong amoeba
watered & trained her on-loan bougainvillea
greeted by bells & firecrackers midnight & dawn
till driven out by flames from enmity's sword
administrators raised against a syndicate strike

then to Austin with its cicadas' rattling whirr
to its soil soon depleted & its humidity high
& yet on Lazy Lane worked tirelessly again

picking from her plot her Kentucky wonders
for nutritious salads shared with whoever came
raising her family through her patience & taste
through the lessons & grades & the bills to pay
earning & learning in light of her nurturing rays
till the landlord notified he would sell his estate
when moved to Irma Drive with its higher rate
where afternoon sun burned her red dianthus
fought losing battles with mounding fire ants
then read in the newspaper of a buy-down plan
an affordable home where could design & plant
those xeriscapes pictured in her library books

& so in Cedar Park would start from scratch
setting out a mountain laurel an Arizona ash
grape vines to climb & a honeysuckle cape
with its long draping deep-orange blooms
trumpeting a tune to hummingbird & bee
with cosmos to shoot up as tall as the roof
our world in her as if named after those
though their flimsy stems in growing so thin
slumped if unsupported by her bamboo sticks
all the days of summer fall winter & spring
sustained by leaning on her quiet strength
her very presence a compost a humus of peat
held or let go as moisture retained or drained
at her whispers to marigolds in accented tones
each rooting deeper to endure a relentless heat
but if talking alone wouldn't bring them along
pinched their heads off so they'd blossom again
for little has flourished from just her words
even knowing better have failed to respond
& not a place have lived has ever come up
to her Chilean earth or the Monets she loves
no venomous vipers had menaced her there
no lilies or haystacks bear brushwork pain

here on Mimosa Pass would come to arrange
pebble paths rub leaves to her heart's content
& through her seedlings to inspire her three
to sniff the pungent sage's pineapple scent
savor rue oregano chervil lavender & mint
but only after we built her redwood frames
for elevating her sandy loam & keeping it in
hauled & spread bags of odoriferous mulch
dug up limestone boulders where beds to go

sank aromatic cedar posts & wetted cement
to erect an arbor for her Champagnale vines
& her rustic lattice for the Old Rose to climb
sawed cedar stakes with their perfumed dust
a ritual readied nostrils for the culinary smells
from her sweet basil baking or boiling indoors
outdoors the fragrance of her chaste-vitex tree
transplanted from beside Granny's double pond
the scene of boyhood games of Tarzan & Jane

now pillowed together on the old four-poster
view pink New Dawn out the bedroom window
its pale subtle blooms a rerun of Granny's yard
shown as if before it had gone to wrack & ruin
yet daily she dreads that recurring nightmare
reappears as if the deadly striped caterpillar
comes to wrap itself in & feed on her leaves
or blue stars of borage extinguished in mud
or a poison ivy or oak on her lamb's-ear skin
have applied the cubes for their soothing cold
yet still she has dreamed of that notice received
must abandon the homestead & rent once more
leave the mums & zinnias have fed & sprayed
blossoms beaks dipped in tongues have licked
rejoicing in her bright-hued throats in hot Julys
nectar stored against January & February sleet
rock-cleared caliche turned with fork & spade
for calendulas blue salvia hollyhocks & yarrow
for vincas portulacas four-o'clocks figs & pears
thyme germander lemon balm dittany of Crete
some do well in winter some in milder weather
a man & woman may in every month & season
as this uprooted other who's honored the native
has braved my arid summers with her santolina
made the best of indigenous wherever it's been
a perennial herself who has flowered each year
more than a garden guide to her tubers & buds
mate & mother who cultivates by her is & does

María in Memoriam (1944-2020)

1

what good is going on with her not here
well-meaning friends say live & write of her
but how can she be served by either act
cremation having with its heartless heat
reduced to ash her smiling lips & teeth
delicious were they once to watch & kiss
her soft brown eyes sweet ears & witty tongue
she now can read or hear or speak with none
whatever could be said to bring them back
not even bones for let her loved ones know
no casket no mortician's painted show
so why seek words to take her features' place
when those rely as much on artifice
as any make-up on her artless face

2

against the best advice I yet persist
in telling friends there just does not exist
a reason to remain without her here
no hands to hold & never more to hear
her reassuring voice as when it said
with only me could she have ever wed
but now the kids both say she never would
have wanted me to fall apart & not
live on & in my grief I have forgot-
ten how her wish had always been to die
before I did & not be left to lie
alone & how she wanted me to go
on writing & remarry too & so
be happy when with only her I could

3

the flowers she had planted still grow on
though weeds & ivy threaten all her beds
where happily I then would rake & dig
but if her salvia pinks & greggii reds
should not survive I shall not feel bereft
for no perennial is worth a fig
with her not coming back year after year
her beauty & her fragrance once so near
now never here yet friends say just go on
keep watering the potted herbs she left
but how can garnish help a frozen meal
so microwaved it smells & looks unreal
her dishes fresh nutritious never plain
no recipe of hers will taste again

4

unjealous strong & wise she was & bright
& yet had married me who never has
had any of her clear-eyed qualities
could not conceive what she had ever seen
in me or how she left her land & came
with me to this has no respect for those
whose veins (as hers did) pulse with Latin blood
when asked at first she offered up the same
tired maxim "love is blind" unfazed in light
of flaw or fault but then had said she judged
that she should join with one could be as keen
as she on books & faithfulness in throes
of woe one stirred & soothed by verse & jazz
her absence though no word or note will ease

5

was all I ever could have wished for in
a friend a love a wife rolled into one
but on first sight thought none of that before
a book checked out from her had let me hear
her speaking with her fetching accent in
her second tongue my rare librarian
with skin so soft & smooth & after more
than fifty years with me still fresh & clear
those cozy chats with her were so much fun
until remembrance ceased & any word
except *Coneja* (sister hers so dear)
seemed even in her Spanish not to mean
a thing & to endearments lipped between
caresses no response since merely heard

6

too late to say the words I would have said
the heavy burden of unspoken love
although expressed so often not enough
no matter if in every different way
as "crazy over" "mad about" "adore"
yet never half the number due each day
in gratitude & homage ever owed
to her who blessed me with her selfless years
so full of warmth & wisdom & bestowed
upon the kids & friends she always touched
by insights shared & facts in books she read
in Spanish English French & far above
those three her own Chilean with its lore
she missed each day brings on remorse's tears

7

how lucky to have lived with her so long
though never had deserved to be with her
as one friend with a crush on her declared
agreed with him & told him so yet said
the choice had been her own if not of fate
since she believed almost that it had brought
together two from cultures poles apart
if differed in our speech were one in thought
a countryman she did for two years date
but in the end had not for him so cared
as for her foreigner she chose instead
who never would fit in nor quite belong
exiled herself for him aware could err
& he turn out unworthy of her heart

8

had never felt could measure up to her
& stood in awe of having been the one
directed to her door by destiny
design or accident or hook or crook
acknowledged each day's prize unfairly won
for knew the others sharp & gifted too
who clearly merited her hand much more
& yet throughout the years I saw I grew
in every way from having been allowed
to sleep with her & though unearned to be
night after night admitted to her store
of intuitions lessons learned from book
or life & taught to me through her own per-
fect bliss made me less cowed of her more proud

9

with her at home could feel the peace within
& all the joy she brought to every room
with prints on walls her knickknacks on the shelves
the photos of the kids & grandkids too
of us with smiles the posters from our trips
to Taos & my local Texas towns
would not have known if had not been for her
insisting we should visit them ourselves
take in a landmark or a famous tomb
the farmer markets with their cider sips
their blushing peaches & their country sounds
from fiddle bands until would come back then
to doors & floors meant more with her astir
now mean much less with only one of two

10

the happiest of all my days was when
she let me take her as my love for life
& not for being just a pretty wife
but one to urge us both to find within
the vital drive for each's highest aims
to reach them then as truly equal mates
united even though sex separates
yet not from fondness nor the newborn names
the saddest came when saw her eyes roll back
& knew she left me with my lesser self
to face the future with this deep regret
for time not spent with her & for my lack
of focus when I had & so much self-
ishness yet loved by her cannot forget

11

our life so wonderful & happy too
a fairy tale from her own point of view
to me beyond belief since hopes for such
had held so few till felt her magic touch
& knew had never been with one like her
for lacking common sense all others were
far less had they approached her loveliness
still less her sincere candid readiness
to take me with my own deficiencies
shortcomings she endured but did her best
to mend the worst while lived with all the rest
would tell our kids your father's idiocies
have been atoned for since he loves & respects
me so yet could not save her from disease

12

can take scant credit for contentment in
her life with me since her own happiness
she made herself in spite of my missteps
her few needs too conduced to that result
now painfully confess of wedding vows
I failed to cherish her in sickness when
(by then our past to her beyond recall)
she fought against a stranger washed her hair
& rinsed shampoo & brushed her teeth till all
my patience lost I yelled at her insult-
ing words a worse incontinence I swear
than hers with diapers changed in our own house
or kneeling worship-like on restroom floors
in filling stations & in grocery stores

13

the one unlucky number some believe
but this thirteenth resolved to look out for
an ending happier than hers had been
so hard to think of that along with loss
of all she was had made for paradise
yet in this grief now read again her note
inside the book she gave in which she wrote
how from the first she knew this love was real
not seeming so as in those times before
with soldier boy & others who had eyes
for her & she for them until had seen
the signs within her heart as in her thoughts
should wait for one would never once deceive
nor ever change as fortune's fickle wheel

14

o how could I have ever said to her
if you will marry me you ought to know
that always poetry comes first with me
why did she not reject me then & there
she would of course replace it soon enough
once all she was & made & said & loved
(as covers for the couches she would sew
her voices for each doll & Pooh the bear
our kids she bore & books she read again)
had filled my verses friends did all prefer
to those I wrote & thought my solid best
her quick assent remains a sweet refrain
reminding how she passed the true-love test
since foolish words were less to her than we

15

she wrote to them to introduce herself
but neither Mom nor Dad replied to her
too jealous of her place in my new life
Aunt Sis did write a slanted florid hand
was hard to read yet so endearing were
her words: Assure your mother everyone
will take good care of you & will demand
my nephew love & always treat you well
He's like a son to me I'm proud to tell
of his accomplishments His very best
will now be you o how could she have guessed
or known before she saw & heard the won-
der of that face & speech of my own wife-
to-be whose depths I barely knew myself

16

had said that I would write of her no more
gave reasons why but then continued to
& in this stiff & worn-out sonnet form
a hypocrite I was when swore before
that I could never live without her near
& yet went on with her no longer here
except in lines that made me feel I knew
verse after verse she kept me company
now let the iambs count & rhymes perform
that words may bring again her quiet charm
that syllables may sing each absent trait
(though each still leaves an emptiness in me)
& may this language somehow reach my mate
to say I grieve for you my Poetry

www.ingramcontent.com/pod-product-compliance
Lightning Source LLC
Chambersburg PA
CBHW031422150426
43191CB00006B/363